REALSIMPLE
meals made easy

WRITTEN BY RENEE SCHETTLER

PHOTOGRAPHS BY ANNA WILLIAMS

REAL**SIMPLE** Time Inc.
HOME ENTERTAINMENT

•••YOU'VE NO DOUBT HEARD THE ADAGE about the unavoidable nature of death and taxes. To that short, onerous list I'd like to add one more thing: making dinner. Even for those of us who like to cook, the routine inevitability of dinner can feel…oppressive. And unlike death and taxes, dinner is something you experience every night. Rain or shine, in good times and bad, accompanied by soft music or the clatter of a baby spoon on a high-chair tray, dinnertime will eventually be upon you. You may be ready, and you may not.

With that in mind, can you think of a more appealing phrase than "easy dinner"? Probably not, considering you've picked up this book. And easy dinner is just what this book delivers. Whether you're looking for a meal that can go from oven to table in 30 minutes (or less), or one that requires very little cleanup (think one pot) or no stove (really), you can turn to any of the six chapters in this book and know that, regardless of what type of night you're having, supper will be solved.

Although the recipes in this collection of *Real Simple* favorites may promise different benefits—after all, there aren't many dishes that both require no cooking and freeze well—they share certain key attributes. They have been rigorously tested, meaning they are easy to follow and virtually foolproof by the time they make it to your kitchen. They take readily available ingredients and combine them in fresh, unexpected ways. And because the ingredients are familiar (read: widely acceptable to all ages), they will be sure to please just about any palate.

I HOPE YOU FIND THIS BOOK a stress-reducing (not to mention beautiful) addition to your kitchen. It will not render death, taxes, or even making dinner avoidable, but it will turn that last activity into something you can actually look forward to. Every day.

Kristin van Ogtrop

Managing Editor, *Real Simple*

contents

one-pot meals

Sometimes preparing dinner can feel like conducting a symphony…on your stovetop. While a motley crew of cookware simultaneously sautés, boils, and stews, you struggle to keep it all in tune. And your reward after the performance? A sinkful of dirty dishes. Perhaps it's time you introduced a few solo acts into your repertoire. The recipes in this chapter require only a single pot, pan, or skillet, making it particularly easy to pull off a flawless performance. Better still, you can leave what minimal cleanup there is to your little percussionists.

ROAST CHICKEN AND VEGETABLES

hands-on time: 30 minutes | total time: 2 hours | makes 4 servings

1 3$\frac{1}{2}$ - to 4-pound chicken

2 teaspoons kosher salt

$\frac{1}{2}$ teaspoon black pepper

2 lemons, halved

1 cup fresh herbs (parsley, tarragon, thyme, rosemary, or sage, in any combination)

3 tablespoons unsalted butter, at room temperature

3 medium yellow onions, cut into $\frac{1}{2}$-inch-thick slices

3 carrots, peeled (and halved lengthwise, if thick)

1$\frac{1}{2}$ pounds Yukon gold or new potatoes, halved (if small) or cut into 1$\frac{1}{2}$-inch chunks (peel first, if desired)

1 head garlic, unpeeled

Heat oven to 425° F. Rinse the chicken inside and out and pat it dry with paper towels. Season the inside with $\frac{1}{2}$ teaspoon of the salt and $\frac{1}{4}$ teaspoon of the pepper. Place the lemons and herbs inside the cavity. Rub the outside of the bird with the butter and season with $\frac{1}{2}$ teaspoon of the salt and the remaining pepper. Place the onions, carrots, potatoes, and garlic in a roasting pan. Season with the remaining salt. Place the chicken on top of the vegetables and roast until the thigh registers 180° F on a meat thermometer, about 1$\frac{1}{2}$ hours. Let the chicken rest on a cutting board for 15 minutes before carving. Meanwhile, using a slotted spoon, transfer the onions, carrots, and potatoes to a platter. Using a large spoon, skim any fat from the surface of the pan juices and discard. Place the roasting pan over medium heat and simmer the pan juices until slightly reduced, about 3 minutes. Transfer the chicken to the platter and serve the pan juices on the side.

••• Tip

If you don't have a roasting pan, use a large ovenproof skillet to roast the chicken. (It's also the perfect size and shape for deep-dish apple pie.)

one-pot meals

BEEF AND BEER STEW

hands-on time: 25 minutes | total time: 3 hours, 15 minutes | makes 6 servings

6 tablespoons olive oil

4 slices bacon, diced

2¹/₂ pounds rump roast or bottom round, cut into 6 equal portions, or 2¹/₂ pounds precut stew meat

¹/₂ teaspoon kosher salt

¹/₄ teaspoon black pepper

4 medium yellow onions, thickly sliced

2 cloves garlic, crushed

1 14.5-ounce can diced tomatoes

2 12-ounce bottles dark beer, such as brown ale

2 tablespoons light brown sugar

1 tablespoon minced fresh thyme or 1 teaspoon dried thyme

1 tablespoon minced fresh rosemary or 1 teaspoon dried rosemary

1¹/₂ pounds Yukon gold potatoes, cut into 1¹/₂-inch chunks (peel first, if desired)

Heat oven to 350° F. Place the oil and bacon in a Dutch oven over medium heat. Fry the bacon until crisp and transfer it to a paper towel–lined plate; set aside. Season the beef with the salt and pepper. Add some of the beef to the pot, being careful not to crowd the pieces. Cook until browned, about 7 minutes per side. Transfer to the plate with the bacon; set aside. Repeat with the remaining beef. Add the onions and garlic to the pot and cook until softened, about 7 minutes. Spoon off and discard any excess fat. Return the beef and bacon to the pot and add the tomatoes, beer, brown sugar, thyme, and rosemary. Bring to a simmer. Cover and transfer to oven. After 10 minutes, check to see if the stew is simmering; if not, increase oven temperature by 25° F. Cook until the meat is falling apart, about 2 hours. Add the potatoes and cook until tender, about 30 minutes more. To serve, ladle the stew into individual bowls.

••• Tip

A Dutch oven may be old-fashioned, but it's not outdated. Use this ovenproof pot with a tight-fitting lid for stews, roasts, braises, and baked beans.

SCALLOP AND CORN CHOWDER

hands-on time: 25 minutes | total time: 50 minutes | makes 4 servings

  5 slices bacon
1 1/2 pounds sea scallops (about 16)
  3/4 teaspoon kosher salt
  1/4 teaspoon black pepper
  1 small yellow onion, thinly
    sliced into half-moons
  1/2 pound Yukon gold potatoes,
    cut into 1/2-inch pieces (peel
    first, if desired)
  1/2 cup dry white wine
  1 cup low-sodium chicken broth
  1/2 cup heavy cream
  1 cup corn kernels, frozen or
    fresh (from 2 ears)
  1/4 cup finely chopped fresh
    flat-leaf parsley leaves

Fry the bacon in a large skillet or stockpot over medium heat until crisp. Transfer to a paper towel–lined plate; set aside. You should have about 2 tablespoons of bacon drippings remaining in the pan (if not, supplement with olive oil). Rinse the scallops and pat them dry with paper towels. Season them with the salt and pepper. Increase heat to medium-high. Add some of the scallops to the pan, being careful not to crowd them. Cook until golden brown, about 2 minutes per side. Transfer to a plate. Repeat with the remaining scallops. Reduce heat to medium. Add the onion to the pan and cook until softened, about 5 minutes. Add the potatoes, wine, broth, and cream. Bring to a simmer. Cover partially and simmer gently until the potatoes are tender, about 20 minutes. Add the scallops and corn and cook for 4 minutes. To serve, ladle into bowls and sprinkle with the parsley and crumbled bacon.

•••Tip

What's the main difference between sea scallops and bay scallops? Their size and origin: Big sea scallops come from the open ocean, while small bay scallops hail from closer to shore.

one-pot meals

VEGETABLE SOUP

hands-on time: 20 minutes | total time: 40 minutes | makes 4 servings

2 tablespoons olive oil

1 large yellow onion, chopped

2 carrots, chopped

2 celery stalks, chopped

3 14.5-ounce cans low-sodium chicken broth

1/2 pound Yukon gold potatoes, cut into 1-inch chunks (peel first, if desired)

1 tablespoon fresh thyme leaves or 1 teaspoon dried thyme

1/2 teaspoon kosher salt

1 14.5-ounce can diced tomatoes

1/4 pound green beans, cut into 1-inch pieces

1 cup chopped broccoli Grated Parmesan (optional)

1 baguette, sliced and toasted (optional)

Heat the oil in a large saucepan or stockpot over medium-high heat. Add the onion, carrots, and celery and cook until softened but not browned, about 5 minutes. Add the broth, 1 cup of water, the potatoes, thyme, and salt. Bring to a boil. Reduce heat, cover partially, and simmer for 15 minutes. Add the tomatoes, beans, and broccoli, return to a simmer, and cook until the vegetables are tender, 5 to 10 minutes. To serve, ladle the soup into bowls. Sprinkle with the Parmesan and serve with the baguette slices, if desired.

and the next time, try...

Making an ad hoc minestrone. When you add the potatoes to the pot, also include one 15-ounce can of cannellini beans (drained), 1/2 a head of cabbage (shredded), and a handful of macaroni or broken spaghetti.

••• **Tip**

When it comes to cooking, the gold standard of potatoes is, well, the Yukon gold. Not only does it have a rich, buttery flavor but it also retains its shape during heating, making it terrific for soups, stews, roasts, and mashes.

ROAST COD WITH CRISP POTATOES

hands-on time: 10 minutes | total time: 50 minutes | makes 6 servings

3 pounds Yukon gold or new
  potatoes, halved (if small) or
  cut into 1$^{1}/_{2}$-inch chunks
  (peel first, if desired)

3 tablespoons plus 2 teaspoons
  olive oil

1 teaspoon kosher salt

$^{1}/_{2}$ teaspoon black pepper

6 6-ounce cod fillets, skin removed
  Zest of $^{1}/_{2}$ lemon, peeled into
  thin strips (optional)

1 tablespoon chopped fresh
  chives (optional)

Heat oven to 450° F. Place the potatoes in a roasting pan or on a baking sheet. Drizzle with 3 tablespoons of the oil and toss to coat. Sprinkle with $^{1}/_{2}$ teaspoon of the salt and $^{1}/_{4}$ teaspoon of the pepper. Roast for 20 minutes. Stir and roast for 10 minutes more. Meanwhile, rinse the cod fillets and pat them dry with paper towels. After the 30 minutes of roasting, move the potatoes to the sides of the pan and place the fillets in the center. Drizzle with the remaining oil and sprinkle with the remaining salt and pepper. Redistribute the potatoes around the fillets. Roast until the fillets are the same color throughout and flake easily, about 10 minutes. Top with the lemon zest and chives (if using).

···Tip

Serve this baked version of fish and chips along with ketchup for the kids and malt vinegar for the adults.

one-pot meals

LAMB TAGINE WITH COUSCOUS

hands-on time: 50 minutes | total time: 2 hours (includes marinating) | makes 6 to 8 servings

2 teaspoons paprika

1/4 teaspoon ground turmeric

1/2 teaspoon ground cumin

1/4 teaspoon ground cayenne

1 teaspoon ground cinnamon

1 teaspoon kosher salt

4 tablespoons olive oil

1 1/2 pounds lamb loin, cut into
1 1/2-inch pieces

1 yellow onion, thickly sliced

4 carrots, peeled into thin strips

1 clove garlic, finely chopped

1 tablespoon grated fresh ginger
Zest of 1/2 lemon, grated

1 32-ounce container low-sodium
chicken broth

1 10-ounce box couscous

1/4 cup fresh cilantro leaves,
roughly chopped

1/4 cup fresh flat-leaf parsley
leaves, roughly chopped

1/4 cup kalamata olives, pitted
and halved

Combine the paprika, turmeric, cumin, cayenne, cinnamon, salt, and 2 tablespoons of the oil in a large resealable bag. Add the lamb, seal, and shake to coat. Refrigerate for at least 1 hour and up to 12. Heat the remaining oil in a large saucepan or Dutch oven over medium heat. Add the onion and carrots. Cook, stirring occasionally, for 15 minutes. Transfer to a plate. Add some of the lamb to the pan, being careful not to crowd the pieces. Brown on all sides, about 12 minutes total. Transfer to a plate. Repeat with the remaining lamb. Return all the lamb to the pot. Add the garlic, ginger, and lemon zest and stir to coat. Return the onion and carrots to the pot, add the broth, and bring to a boil. Stir in the couscous. Remove from heat, cover, and let rest for 10 minutes. Stir in the cilantro, parsley, and olives. Divide among individual bowls.

and the next time, try...
Cutting the cooking time in half by using leftover chicken or turkey. Instead of coating the meat with the spices, just add the spices to the oil with the garlic, ginger, and zest. Then add the meat when you stir in the couscous.

···Tip
If you can't find loin of lamb, ask your butcher to cut a leg of lamb into 1 1/2-inch pieces. Although relatively expensive, these cuts cook quickly and are very tender.

BAKED BEANS

hands-on time: 15 minutes | total time: 17 hours (includes soaking) | makes 6 to 8 servings

1 pound dry navy or soldier beans

1/3 cup molasses

1/3 cup cider vinegar

1 teaspoon dry mustard

1/2 cup dark brown sugar, firmly packed

1/4 teaspoon black pepper

1 large white onion, quartered

1/4 pound salt pork or bacon, cut into 1 1/2-inch chunks
    Buttered bread, such as Boston brown or a hearty whole-grain, for serving

Place the beans in a large ovenproof pot or Dutch oven. Add enough water to cover by 3 inches and let stand for at least 10 hours. Drain the beans and return them to the pot. Add just enough water to cover the beans. Bring to a boil, then reduce heat and simmer gently until the beans are softened, about 1 hour. (Add water periodically as necessary to keep the beans barely covered.) Meanwhile, in a medium bowl, whisk together the molasses, vinegar, mustard, brown sugar, pepper, and 2 tablespoons of water. Drain the beans. Place the onion in the empty pot. Top with the beans, then the salt pork or bacon, then the molasses mixture. Heat oven to 300° F. Cover the pot tightly and bake until the beans are tender, the bacon is falling apart, and the liquid is thick and bubbling, about 6 hours. Check the beans during the last hour of cooking; if they appear to be drying out, add more water (or even a second batch of the molasses mixture). Spoon the beans into individual bowls and serve with the buttered bread.

••• Tip

Salt pork is similar to bacon—it's just thicker, fattier, and unsmoked. Look for it near the bacon in the supermarket.

one-pot meals

ROAST SALMON, FENNEL, AND RED ONION

hands-on time: 10 minutes | total time: 45 minutes | makes 4 servings

2 small fennel bulbs, cut into
  1/2-inch wedges
1 large red onion, cut into
  1/2-inch wedges
6 cloves garlic
1 cup cherry or grape tomatoes
1/2 bunch fresh thyme sprigs
1 teaspoon kosher salt
1/2 teaspoon black pepper
2 teaspoons olive oil
4 6-ounce salmon fillets,
  skin removed
1 lemon, halved

Heat oven to 400° F. Place the fennel, onion, garlic, tomatoes, thyme sprigs, 1/2 teaspoon of the salt, 1/4 teaspoon of the pepper, and the oil in a roasting pan or 9-by-13-inch baking dish and toss to coat. Spread evenly and roast for 20 minutes. Meanwhile, rinse the salmon fillets and pat them dry with paper towels. Move the vegetables to the sides of the pan and place the fillets in the center. Redistribute the vegetables around the fillets. Squeeze the lemon over the top, then sprinkle with the remaining salt and pepper. Return to oven and roast until the fillets are the same color throughout and flake easily, about 10 to 12 minutes. To serve, transfer the fillets and vegetables to individual plates.

••• Tip

To remove burnt-on food from a roasting pan or a baking dish, add a generous pinch of baking soda before filling it with warm water. Then set it aside to soak for at least 1 hour before washing.

CHICKEN CACCIATORE

hands-on time: 45 minutes | total time: 1 hour, 50 minutes | makes 4 servings

1/4 cup all-purpose flour

1 1/4 teaspoons kosher salt

3/4 teaspoon black pepper

1 3 1/2- to 4-pound chicken, cut into pieces

1/4 cup olive oil

1 medium yellow onion, roughly chopped

1 carrot, diced

1 celery stalk, diced

4 cloves garlic, finely chopped

3 sprigs fresh thyme

1 bay leaf

1 28-ounce can plum tomatoes

1/3 cup dry red wine

1/4 cup chopped fresh flat-leaf parsley leaves

In a shallow bowl, combine the flour, 1 teaspoon of the salt, and 1/2 teaspoon of the pepper. Rinse the chicken and pat it dry with paper towels. Working in batches, lightly coat the chicken in the flour mixture, shaking off any excess. Heat the oil in a Dutch oven or large saucepan over medium heat. Add some of the chicken to the pan, being careful not to crowd the pieces. Cook the chicken until browned, 4 to 5 minutes per side. Transfer to a plate; set aside. Repeat with the remaining chicken. Add the onion to the pan and cook for 2 minutes. Add the carrot, celery, garlic, thyme, and bay leaf. Cook, stirring occasionally, for 10 minutes. Crush the tomatoes in the can with a large spoon and stir them into the vegetables. Add the wine and the remaining salt and pepper and bring to a simmer. Add the chicken, reduce heat, and cover. Simmer for 45 minutes, turning the pieces occasionally. Remove and discard the bay leaf. Stir in the parsley and serve on individual plates.

••• Tip

If you have a difficult time adjusting the flame on your stovetop so it maintains a gentle simmer, try stacking two burner grates, one on top of the other (just make absolutely sure that one fits securely over the other and that they are stable and level). The second grate will act as a buffer for a flame that is a little too hot.

one-pot meals

CREAMY PARMESAN RISOTTO

hands-on time: 40 minutes | total time: 45 minutes | makes 4 servings

4 tablespoons unsalted butter

1 medium yellow onion, finely chopped

1 clove garlic, finely chopped

1 1/2 cups Arborio rice

1 cup dry white wine

4 cups low-sodium chicken broth

1/2 teaspoon kosher salt

1/4 teaspoon black pepper

1/2 cup (2 ounces) grated Parmesan, plus more for serving

Melt 2 tablespoons of the butter in a medium saucepan over medium heat. Add the onion and garlic and cook, stirring with a wooden spoon, until the onion is softened, about 5 minutes. Add the rice and cook, stirring constantly, until it is coated with butter and begins to turn translucent, about 2 minutes. Add the wine and cook, stirring frequently, until all the liquid is absorbed, 3 to 5 minutes. Meanwhile, pour the broth into a medium bowl and microwave on high until hot but not boiling. Ladle 1/2 cup of the warm broth into the rice mixture. Simmer, stirring occasionally, until the broth is absorbed. Repeat, adding 1/2 cup of the broth at a time, until the rice is cooked through but still firm. This should take 20 to 25 minutes total (you may need to reheat the broth once during this time). Remove from heat and add the salt, pepper, Parmesan, and the remaining butter. Stir to combine. Serve immediately with additional Parmesan on the side.

••• Tip

Contrary to common kitchen lore, it's not necessary to stir risotto constantly. Frequent stirring is required at the beginning to coax the rice to creaminess. But after you've added the first ladleful or two of broth, an occasional stir will suffice.

STEAMED HALIBUT AND ASPARAGUS IN PARCHMENT

hands-on time: 25 minutes | total time: 50 minutes | makes 4 servings

1½ pounds small red potatoes,
    sliced about ¼ inch thick

4 6-ounce halibut fillets, skin
    re-moved

2 teaspoons kosher salt

1 teaspoon black pepper

2 tablespoons chopped fresh
    tarragon

4 scallions, trimmed and cut
    into 1-inch pieces

1 pound asparagus, trimmed and
    cut into 1-inch pieces

1 tablespoon extra-virgin olive oil

Parchment paper, cut into
8 15-by-15-inch sheets

Heat oven to 400° F. Divide 4 of the parchment paper sheets between 2 baking sheets. (The paper sheets may overlap slightly.) Place ¼ of the potatoes in the center of each sheet. Rinse the halibut fillets and pat them dry with paper towels. Place the fillets on top of the potatoes. Season with the salt and pepper. Add the tarragon, scallions, and asparagus. Drizzle with the oil. Top with the remaining parchment paper sheets and fold the edges over several times to seal. Bake for 25 minutes. (Although you can't check for doneness, this is ample time for the fish and potatoes to cook through.) To serve, place a packet on each plate and cut open.

and the next time, try...
Using almost anything that swims in place of the halibut. Salmon, tuna, and cod all work just fine and cook in about the same amount of time.

••• Tip
If the folded edge of a parchment packet starts to unfold, place half a lemon or a carrot on the offending seam to keep it flat while baking.

one-pot meals

ROAST CHICKEN WITH OLIVES AND THYME

hands-on time: 25 minutes | total time: 2 hours, 25 minutes (includes marinating) | makes 4 servings

1 3^1/$_2$- to 4-pound chicken,
   cut into pieces
1 teaspoon honey
1 small shallot, finely chopped
^{1}/$_2$ cup extra-virgin olive oil
1^1/$_2$ teaspoons kosher salt
1 teaspoon black pepper
   Zest of 1 lemon, peeled in
   thin strips
^{1}/$_4$ cup fresh lemon juice
1 cup kalamata olives, pitted
5 cloves garlic, thinly sliced
1 small bunch fresh thyme sprigs
1 small head cauliflower, cut into
   florets (optional)

Rinse the chicken and pat it dry with paper towels. Place it in a roasting pan or 9-by-13-inch baking dish. In a small bowl, combine the honey, shallot, oil, 1 teaspoon of the salt, ^{1}/$_4$ teaspoon of the pepper, lemon zest and juice, olives, and garlic. Pour the lemon mixture over the chicken and turn to coat. Scatter the thyme sprigs over the top. Refrigerate, covered, for at least 1 hour or overnight. Heat oven to 425° F. Season the chicken with the remaining salt and pepper. Place the cauliflower (if using) around the chicken and spoon the lemon mixture over the top. Roast until the chicken is golden brown, about 20 minutes. Reduce heat to 375° F. Continue to roast until the chicken is cooked through, about 40 minutes more. Spoon the olives and pan juices over the chicken and serve.

•••Tip
Roasting chicken pieces, as opposed to an entire chicken, takes slightly less time and spares you the hassle of carving.

CHAPTER TWO

no-shop meals

It's your third time scavenging through the fridge, the freezer, and the cabinets, helplessly hoping that *something* will materialize for dinner and spare you a trip to the store. Yet all you've turned up is a box of pasta, a stray jalapeño, and one-sixteenth of a bag of frozen peas. Not exactly the makings of a proper meal—or so it would appear. Next time you need to conjure something out of nothing, take a quick inventory of the recipes on the following pages. Then check the pantry again. Dinner is in there, if you know where to look.

FLUFFY CORN AND GOAT CHEESE OMELETS

hands-on time: 25 minutes | total time: 30 minutes | makes 2 servings

  6 eggs, separated
1/2 teaspoon kosher salt
1/4 teaspoon black pepper
  1 cup corn kernels, frozen or
     fresh (from 2 ears)
  2 tablespoons unsalted butter
1/2 cup (2 ounces) goat cheese,
     crumbled
  8 fresh chives, chopped

In a large bowl, whisk together the egg yolks, salt, pepper, and corn. In a separate bowl, using an electric mixer on medium, beat the egg whites until soft peaks form. With a spatula, gently fold the egg whites into the yolk mixture until no trace of white remains. Melt 1 tablespoon of the butter in a nonstick skillet over medium heat. Pour in half of the egg mixture. Cook, without stirring, until the eggs barely begin to set, about 1 minute. Use the spatula to lift the edge of the omelet so the uncooked egg flows underneath. Cook, still without stirring, until the top is almost completely set, about 2 minutes. Sprinkle 1/3 of the cheese and 1/3 of the chives over half the omelet. Using the spatula, fold the other half of the omelet over the filling. Cook until set. Tilt the skillet and slide the omelet onto a plate. Repeat with the remaining butter, egg mixture, and half the remaining cheese and chives. Sprinkle the omelets with the remaining cheese and chives. Serve immediately.

•••Tip

When you cook omelets, use a skillet that doesn't have a plastic or wooden handle. That way, if the eggs are still runny on top but are beginning to brown on the bottom, you can stick the skillet under the broiler for about 30 seconds to set the eggs before folding the omelet.

no-shop meals

TUNA AND WHITE BEAN SALAD

hands-on time: 15 minutes | total time: 15 minutes | makes 4 servings

2 6-ounce cans tuna, drained

1 15-ounce can cannellini beans, drained and rinsed

1 12-ounce jar roasted red peppers, drained and roughly chopped

2 tablespoons capers

Zest of 1 lemon, grated

1 tomato, roughly chopped (optional)

3 tablespoons fresh lemon juice

1 tablespoon extra-virgin olive oil

$1/2$ teaspoon kosher salt

$1/2$ teaspoon black pepper

Toasted bread, such as pita, for serving

In a large bowl, combine the tuna, beans, red peppers, capers, lemon zest, and tomato (if using). In a separate bowl, whisk together the lemon juice, oil, salt, and black pepper. Pour the vinaigrette over the tuna mixture and toss. Serve with the bread.

and the next time, try...

Improvising with whatever kitchen staples you have on hand:

• Olives

• Red onion

• Chickpeas

• Celery

• Fresh basil or flat-leaf parsley

• Jarred artichokes

• Balsamic vinegar

• Cooked rice

···•Tip

Stash a couple of cans of Italian tuna packed in olive oil in your cabinet for emergencies. The tuna's robust—but not tinny— taste makes it a great go-to for salads, sandwiches, and pasta dishes.

PARMESAN-CRUSTED CHICKEN CUTLETS

hands-on time: 20 minutes | total time: 30 minutes | makes 4 servings

2 large eggs

1 tablespoon Dijon mustard (optional)

2 1/4 cups (9 ounces) finely grated Parmesan

1 cup dried bread crumbs

1/2 teaspoon kosher salt

1/4 teaspoon black pepper

1 to 1 1/2 pounds chicken cutlets

6 tablespoons olive oil

1 head Boston or butter lettuce

1 lemon, cut into wedges

In a shallow bowl, whisk together the eggs and mustard (if using). In a separate bowl, combine 2 cups of the Parmesan, the bread crumbs, salt, and pepper. Rinse the chicken and pat it dry with paper towels. Dip one of the cutlets into the egg mixture, allowing any excess to drip off, then coat it in the bread-crumb mixture. Transfer to a plate. Repeat with the remaining chicken, batter, and bread-crumb mixture. Heat 2 tablespoons of the oil in a nonstick skillet over medium-high heat. Add half of the cutlets. Cook, turning once, until browned and cooked through, 3 to 5 minutes per side. Transfer to a plate. Carefully wipe out the skillet, add 2 more tablespoons of the oil, and repeat with the remaining cutlets. Divide the cutlets and lettuce leaves among individual plates. Drizzle the lettuce with the remaining oil and sprinkle with the remaining Parmesan. Serve the lemon wedges on the side.

••• Tip

If you'd rather not spend the extra money for thin cutlets, you can substitute chicken breasts as long as you flatten them to an even thinness. Place them in between 2 pieces of plastic wrap and roll or pound them using a rolling pin, a meat pounder, a heavy skillet, or even a wine bottle.

no-shop meals

PASTA WITH PEAS AND LEMON

hands-on time: 15 minutes | total time: 25 minutes | makes 4 servings

1 pound dry spaghetti or
  fettuccine
3 tablespoons olive oil
4 cloves garlic, thinly sliced
2 jalapeños, seeded and thinly
  sliced (optional)
  Zest of 1 lemon, grated
1/3 cup fresh lemon juice
1 1/2 cups frozen peas, thawed
  (or less, if it's all you have)
1 teaspoon kosher salt
1/8 teaspoon black pepper
1/3 cup (2 ounces) grated
  Parmesan (optional)

Cook the pasta according to the package directions. Meanwhile, heat 2 tablespoons of the oil in a large skillet over medium-low heat. Add the garlic, jalapeños (if using), and lemon zest and cook until the garlic is golden but not browned, 4 to 5 minutes. Drain the pasta and add it to the skillet with the lemon juice, peas, salt, pepper, and the remaining oil. Heat until warmed through, 3 to 4 minutes. Transfer the pasta to individual plates and sprinkle with the Parmesan (if using).

and the next time, try...
Reaching for angel-hair pasta, capellini, or vermicelli. The thinner strands cook in a fraction of the time thicker pastas take.

••• **Tip**
The amount of juice you can squeeze from a lemon varies significantly. Assume you'll get no less than 2 tablespoons, no more than 4.

CHEDDAR FRENCH TOAST WITH SIZZLED TOMATOES

hands-on time: 35 minutes | total time: 45 minutes | makes 4 to 8 servings

2 large eggs

$1^1/_2$ cups heavy cream or milk

$^3/_4$ teaspoon kosher salt

$1^1/_2$ cups (6 ounces) grated sharp
Cheddar

1 tablespoon fresh thyme leaves
or 1 teaspoon dried thyme
(optional)

8 thick slices country-style bread

4 tablespoons unsalted butter

2 red or green tomatoes,
thickly sliced

$^1/_2$ teaspoon black pepper

1 tablespoon olive oil

With a fork, combine the eggs, cream or milk, and $^1/_2$ teaspoon of the salt in a baking dish. Add the Cheddar and thyme (if using). Soak 2 of the bread slices in the batter for 1 or 2 minutes, turning them once. Meanwhile, melt 1 tablespoon of the butter in a large nonstick skillet over medium heat. With a spatula, lift the bread from the bowl, allowing any excess batter to drip off, and transfer it to the skillet. Use a fork to transfer some of the cheese from the batter to the bread. Cook the bread until golden, 3 to 4 minutes per side. Transfer to a plate and cover to keep warm. Wipe out the skillet with a paper towel. Repeat with the remaining butter, bread, and batter. Season the tomatoes with the remaining salt and the pepper. Wipe out the skillet and return to medium heat. Heat the oil. Add the tomatoes and cook for 2 minutes per side. Serve alongside the French toast.

•••Tip

Use a loaf of sturdy, preferably day-old, country-style or Italian bread when you make French toast. Light, fluffy baguettes and sliced sandwich breads tend to become soggy.

no-shop meals

SALSA QUESADILLAS

hands-on time: 15 minutes | total time: 25 minutes | makes 4 servings

8 8-inch flour tortillas

2 cups (8 ounces) grated mozzarella
  or Monterey Jack

1 14- to 16-ounce jar store-bought
  salsa, drained
  Several leaves fresh basil or
  cilantro (optional)

4 teaspoons olive oil

Arrange 4 of the tortillas on a work surface. Divide the mozzarella, salsa, and herbs (if using) among the tortillas, leaving a 1-inch border. Top with the remaining tortillas. Heat the oil in a skillet over medium heat. Cook one quesadilla at a time, turning once, until the cheese melts and the tortillas are crisp and golden, about 2 minutes per side. Transfer to a cutting board. Repeat with the remaining quesadillas. Cut into wedges and serve.

and the next time, try...
Serving up more surprising versions of this no-fail family favorite:
• Make breakfast quesadillas with peanut
  butter, banana, and honey.
• Turn them into a gooey dessert with a generous
  smear of Nutella.
• Take advantage of Thanksgiving leftovers by
  layering turkey, mashed potatoes, some cheese,
  and a spoonful of cranberry sauce.

••• Tip
To save time, broil the quesadillas all together. Arrange them on a baking sheet, brush the tops with olive oil, and broil, turning once, until the cheese melts and the tortillas are golden brown.

SAUCY EGGS

hands-on time: 5 minutes | total time: 15 minutes | makes 2 to 4 servings

1 24- to 26-ounce jar pasta sauce
4 large eggs
1/4 teaspoon kosher salt
1/4 teaspoon black pepper (optional)
Chopped fresh basil leaves
(optional)
Cooked pasta or thickly sliced
bread (optional)

Bring the pasta sauce to a simmer in a large skillet over medium heat. Break one of the eggs into a small dish. Hold the dish close to the skillet and carefully tip the egg into the sauce. Repeat with the remaining eggs. If you want runny yolks, leave the tops of the eggs uncovered; if you prefer firm yolks, spoon some of the sauce over the top. Cover the skillet, reduce heat, and simmer for 10 to 12 minutes. Season with the salt and pepper (if using). Sprinkle with the basil and serve with the pasta or bread, if desired.

and the next time, try...
Fancying up this no-frills recipe:
• Sauté some garlic or onions, or both, in olive
  oil before adding the pasta sauce.
• Throw in some olives or capers when you
  add the pasta sauce.
• Sprinkle with grated Parmesan or Pecorino
  just before serving.

···Tip
**Consider splurging
on a pricey jarred pasta
sauce. When dinner
consists of just 2 or 3
ingredients, each one
counts.**

no-shop meals

CRISPED LEFTOVER PASTA

hands-on time: 10 minutes | total time: 25 minutes | makes 1 to 2 servings

About 4 ounces cooked, unsauced spaghetti or fettuccine, cold

2 teaspoons olive oil

3 slices prosciutto or 2 slices bacon, (optional)

1/4 teaspoon red pepper flakes (optional)

1/4 cup (1 ounce) grated Parmesan, plus more for serving

1/4 teaspoon kosher salt

1/8 teaspoon black pepper

Let the pasta sit at room temperature until it becomes pliable, about 10 minutes. Meanwhile, heat the oil in a nonstick skillet over medium heat. Add the prosciutto or bacon (if using) and cook until crisp. Transfer to a paper towel–lined plate. Drain off and discard all but 2 teaspoons of the drippings in the skillet. Sprinkle the red pepper flakes (if using) over the remaining drippings. Increase heat to medium-high. Add the pasta to the skillet and gently spread it out to form a large nest. Cook, without stirring, until the pasta begins to crisp and brown on the bottom, 4 to 5 minutes. Sprinkle with the Parmesan and prosciutto or bacon (if using). Cook, still without stirring, for about 2 more minutes. Season with the salt and black pepper. Slide or invert the pasta onto a plate and sprinkle with additional Parmesan. Cut into wedges, if desired.

···Tip
Store leftover spaghetti on a dinner plate covered with plastic wrap. This creates a perfect-size nest of noodles that you can slide straight into the skillet.

CHAPTER THREE

30-minute meals

Sure, Einstein devoted two whole theories to the relativity of time. But the only evidence *you* need is that your half-hour commute seems interminable—yet the 30 minutes you have to prepare dinner go by at warp speed. On those far-too-frequent evenings when you're in a race with the clock, rely on these genius recipes, all guaranteed to be on the table in a half hour or less. They may not make time slow down, but they do make every second count.

STEAK WITH ROOT VEGETABLES

hands-on time: 30 minutes | total time: 30 minutes | makes 4 servings

4 8-ounce New York, strip, or
   sirloin steaks, about 1 inch thick

2 teaspoons kosher salt

1/2 teaspoon black pepper

3 tablespoons olive oil

2 carrots, cut lengthwise into
   thin strips

2 parsnips, cut lengthwise into
   thin strips

2 beets, cut into thin slices

1 tablespoon chopped
   fresh tarragon

Season the steaks with 1¹/₂ teaspoons of the salt and ¹/₄ teaspoon of the pepper. Heat 1 tablespoon of the oil in a large skillet over medium-high heat. Add some of the steaks to the skillet and cook to the desired doneness, about 4 minutes per side for medium-rare. Transfer to a plate and cover loosely with foil. Repeat with the remaining steaks. Let rest. Meanwhile, wipe out the skillet with paper towels. Heat the remaining oil over medium-low heat. Add the carrots, parsnips, and beets and cook until tender, 5 to 7 minutes. Season with the remaining salt and pepper and the tarragon. Serve the vegetables alongside the steaks.

and the next time, try...
Substituting any root vegetable for the carrots, parsnips, or beets. Rutabagas and sweet potatoes work particularly well.

••• Tip
To shave a few minutes off this recipe, slice the carrots and parsnips horizontally into thin coins rather than lengthwise into thin strips.

30-minute meals

LINGUINE WITH ARTICHOKES AND LEEKS

hands-on time: 25 minutes | total time: 30 minutes | makes 4 servings

1 pound dry linguine or fettuccine

2 medium leeks (white and light green parts only), rinsed

2 12-ounce jars artichoke hearts (packed in oil), drained

3 tablespoons olive oil

1 tablespoon fresh lemon juice

3 teaspoons kosher salt

1 teaspoon black pepper

1/2 cup (2 ounces) grated Parmesan

Cook the pasta according to the package directions. Meanwhile, halve the leeks lengthwise and thickly slice them crosswise. Halve the artichokes lengthwise. Heat the oil in a large skillet over medium-low heat. Add the leeks and cook, stirring frequently, until softened but not browned, about 5 minutes. Transfer to a plate; set aside. Increase heat to medium and add the artichokes. Cook for 3 minutes per side. Add the leeks, lemon juice, salt, and pepper and toss. Transfer to a large bowl. Drain the pasta. Add it and 1/4 cup of the Parmesan to the vegetables and toss. Serve with the remaining Parmesan on the side.

••• Tip
Leeks tend to trap quite a lot of sand between their layers. To get rid of the grit, halve them, place them in a large bowl of cold water, and swirl. Then wait for a minute. After the dirt settles, lift the leeks out.

GRILLED SHRIMP TACOS

hands-on time: 30 minutes | total time: 30 minutes | makes 4 servings

1/2 cup sour cream

3 tablespoons mayonnaise

3 tablespoons milk

1/2 teaspoon ground cumin

3 tablespoons unsalted butter, melted

2 cloves garlic, finely chopped

1 1/2 pounds large shrimp, peeled and deveined

4 limes, quartered

1/2 teaspoon kosher salt

8 6-inch corn tortillas

3 cups shredded green cabbage

1 14- to 16-ounce jar green (tomatillo) salsa

Wooden skewers, soaked in water for at least 30 minutes

In a small bowl, whisk together the sour cream, mayonnaise, milk, and cumin; set aside. In a separate bowl, combine the butter and garlic. Heat a grill or broiler. Rinse the shrimp and pat them dry with paper towels. Place the shrimp and lime wedges on the skewers. Brush the shrimp with the garlic butter. Grill or broil until the shrimp are cooked through and the limes are browned, about 3 minutes per side. Season the shrimp with the salt. Transfer to a plate. Grill or broil the tortillas until warmed, about 30 seconds per side. Place them between clean towels to keep warm. To serve, remove the shrimp from the skewers, divide them evenly among the tortillas, and top each with the cabbage, sour cream mixture, and salsa. Serve the lime wedges on the side.

•••Tip

Skewer your shrimp twice—that way, they'll lie flat on the grill and won't spin when you turn them. First spear the shrimp through the tail, then bend the shrimp and spear it through the head.

30-minute meals

GRILLED TUNA WITH TOMATO SALSA

hands-on time: 15 minutes | total time: 25 minutes | makes 4 servings

Zest of 1 lemon, grated
3 tablespoons fresh lemon juice
1 teaspoon honey
1 small shallot, finely chopped
1 clove garlic, finely chopped
1 tablespoon fresh oregano
 or 2 teaspoons dried oregano
1/2 cup extra-virgin olive oil
1/2 teaspoon kosher salt
1/4 teaspoon black pepper
4 6- to 8-ounce tuna steaks
2 tomatoes, seeded (if desired)
 and diced
2 tablespoons capers,
 roughly chopped
1 cup arugula, roughly chopped

In a medium bowl, whisk together the lemon zest and juice, honey, shallot, garlic, and oregano. Whisking constantly, slowly add the oil in a steady stream. Season with the salt and pepper. Rinse the tuna steaks and pat them dry with paper towels. Arrange them in a baking dish and drizzle with 1/2 cup of the lemon mixture. Turn to coat. Heat a grill or grill pan on high. Transfer the tuna to the grill or pan. Cook to the desired doneness, about 4 minutes per side for medium-rare. Meanwhile, to make the tomato salsa, add the tomatoes, capers, and arugula to the remaining lemon mixture and toss. Serve the salsa with the tuna.

and the next time, try...
Drizzling the lemon mixture over cooked chicken cutlets or pork chops. It's a faster—and even more flavorful—alternative to marinating.

•••Tip
To seed a tomato, cut it in half crosswise and grasp half in your hand, cut-side down. Hold it over a sink and flick your wrist sharply several times. The seeds should fly right out.

CHICKEN CUTLETS WITH HERB SAUCE

hands-on time: 10 minutes | total time: 30 minutes | makes 4 servings

1 tablespoon olive oil

1½ pounds Yukon gold or new potatoes, cut into ½-inch pieces (peel first, if desired)

1½ teaspoons kosher salt

1 to 1½ pounds chicken cutlets

¼ teaspoon black pepper

¼ cup dry white wine

2 tablespoons unsalted butter, chilled

2 tablespoons chopped fresh herbs, such as rosemary, chives, parsley, or tarragon

Heat oven to 425° F. Heat the oil in a large skillet over medium-high heat. Add the potatoes and cook, stirring occasionally, until golden, about 15 minutes. Transfer to a baking dish and season with 1 teaspoon of the salt. Bake for 10 minutes. Meanwhile, rinse the chicken and pat it dry with paper towels. Season on both sides with ¼ teaspoon of the salt and ⅛ teaspoon of the pepper. Return the skillet to medium-high heat. Add the chicken and cook until browned on each side and cooked through, 3 to 4 minutes per side. Transfer the chicken to a platter. Add the wine to the skillet, reduce heat, and simmer for 2 minutes, constantly stirring and scraping the bottom. Add 1 tablespoon of the butter and stir or whisk until completely combined. Repeat with the remaining butter. Remove the skillet from heat. Add the herbs and the remaining salt and pepper and whisk to combine. Add the potatoes to the platter with the chicken and spoon the sauce over the top.

••• Tip

Want the secret to a smooth, silky sauce? Use cold butter and slowly whisk it into the pan sauce. If you use room-temperature butter, it won't emulsify as nicely.

30-minute meals

PORK CHOPS WITH LEMONY BREAD CRUMBS

hands-on time: 20 minutes | total time: 30 minutes | makes 4 servings

3 tablespoons extra-virgin olive oil
8 thin-cut pork chops
3 teaspoons kosher salt
1/2 teaspoon black pepper
1 14- to 16-ounce jar pasta sauce
1/2 cup dry bread crumbs
2 tablespoons chopped fresh sage
Zest of 1 lemon, grated
1 clove garlic, crushed
1/2 pound green beans
1 1/2 cups arugula
1 tablespoon fresh lemon juice

Heat oven to 350° F. Heat 1 tablespoon of the oil in a large ovenproof skillet over medium-high heat. Season the pork with 1/2 teaspoon of the salt and 1/4 teaspoon of the pepper. Cook until browned but not cooked through, about 2 minutes per side. Remove skillet from heat. Spoon the pasta sauce over the pork. In a small bowl, combine the bread crumbs, sage, lemon zest, garlic, 1/2 teaspoon of the salt, and the remaining pepper. Sprinkle the bread-crumb mixture evenly over the sauce. Transfer the skillet to oven and roast until the sauce is bubbling, about 10 minutes. Meanwhile, bring a large pot of water and the remaining salt to a boil. Add the beans, return to a boil, and cook until tender, 3 to 5 minutes. Drain and transfer to a bowl of ice water. Drain again and return to the bowl. Add the arugula, lemon juice, and the remaining oil and toss. Serve the salad alongside the pork.

••• Tip
You can use plain canned tomato sauce in place of the jarred pasta sauce if that's all you have in your cupboard. It will just make a slightly less rich sauce.

CHICKEN SOUVLAKI

hands-on time: 25 minutes | total time: 30 minutes | makes 4 servings

4 pieces flat bread or pitas
2¹/₂ teaspoons red wine vinegar
1 tablespoon fresh lemon juice
1¹/₂ tablespoons fresh oregano
   or 1¹/₂ teaspoons dried oregano
1¹/₂ tablespoons fresh thyme
   or 1¹/₂ teaspoons dried thyme
¹/₄ teaspoon black pepper
¹/₄ cup extra-virgin olive oil
2 medium tomatoes, cut
   into wedges
¹/₂ small red onion, thinly sliced
³/₄ cup (3 ounces) crumbled Feta
¹/₄ cup kalamata olives, pitted
   if desired
4 boneless, skinless chicken breast
   halves, cut into 4-inch pieces
¹/₂ cup plain yogurt
1 small cucumber, roughly
   chopped (peel first, if desired)
1¹/₂ tablespoons finely chopped
   fresh dill

Heat oven to 250° F. Wrap the bread in foil and place in oven to warm. Meanwhile, in a large bowl, combine 1¹/₂ teaspoons of the vinegar, the lemon juice, oregano, thyme, and pepper. Whisking constantly, slowly add the oil in a steady stream. In a separate bowl, combine the tomatoes, onion, Feta, and olives. Pour 2¹/₂ tablespoons of the vinaigrette over the tomato mixture and toss; set aside. Rinse the chicken and pat it dry with paper towels. Add it to the remaining vinaigrette and toss. Heat a grill or broiler on high. Cook the chicken, turning occasionally, until cooked through, 5 to 7 minutes total. Meanwhile, combine the yogurt, cucumber, dill, and the remaining vinegar in a bowl. Spoon some of the cucumber mixture onto each piece of bread and top with the chicken and the tomato salad.

and the next time, try...
Preparing the souvlaki the traditional way—with lamb. You can also use turkey or shrimp.

•••Tip
For an extra-thick and creamy spread, drain the yogurt to remove excess liquid. Place a paper towel–lined strainer over a bowl, spoon in the yogurt, then refrigerate for at least 20 minutes.

30-minute meals

SOY-GLAZED SALMON WITH NOODLES

hands-on time: 30 minutes | total time: 30 minutes | makes 4 servings

1/2 pound green beans, sliced in
    half lengthwise
1 pound soba noodles or
    whole-wheat spaghetti
1/2 cup plus 3 tablespoons low-
    sodium soy sauce
1 clove garlic, finely chopped
1 tablespoon finely grated
    ginger, plus 2 tablespoons thinly
    sliced ginger
2 tablespoons rice wine, sherry,
    or white wine
4 6-ounce salmon fillets,
    skin removed
3 scallions, cut into 2-inch pieces
1/4 cup rice vinegar
2 tablespoons fresh lemon juice
1 tablespoon granulated sugar

Heat oven to 400° F. Bring a large pot of water to a boil. Add the beans and cook until tender, about 2 minutes. Using a slotted spoon, transfer the beans to a bowl of ice water. Drain and set aside. Add the noodles to the boiling water and cook according to the package directions. Meanwhile, in a baking dish, combine 3 tablespoons of the soy sauce, the garlic, grated ginger, and 1 tablespoon of the wine. Rinse the salmon and pat it dry with paper towels. Add it to the baking dish and turn to coat. Scatter the sliced ginger and scallions over the top. Cover with foil and bake until the fish is the same color throughout and flakes easily, about 20 minutes. Meanwhile, in a small saucepan, combine the vinegar, lemon juice, sugar, and the remaining soy sauce and wine, stirring until the sugar dissolves. Bring to a boil and cook until reduced by half, about 3 minutes. Remove from heat and cover to keep warm. Divide the drained noodles and beans among individual plates, top each with a salmon fillet, and drizzle with the glaze.

···•Tip
If you ask nicely, most fishmongers will remove the skin from a fish fillet for you. If you forget—or yours refuses—grab hold of one edge of the fish, place a knife between the skin and the flesh, and run the blade along the length of the fillet. To prevent your fingers from slipping, grasp the fish through a paper towel.

SOY-MARINATED LONDON BROIL

hands-on time: 15 minutes | total time: 25 minutes | makes 4 servings

1/2 cup low-sodium soy sauce
1/4 cup light brown sugar,
   firmly packed
  1 clove garlic, thinly sliced
1 1/2 pounds top round London
   broil, about 1 1/2 inches thick
1/2 teaspoon black pepper
  8 scallions, trimmed
   Cooked white rice
  1 tablespoon sesame seeds

In a large saucepan, off the heat, combine the soy sauce, brown sugar, and garlic, stirring until the sugar dissolves. Rinse the meat and pat it dry with paper towels. Add the meat to the marinade and turn to coat. (If you have the time, you can cover the saucepan and refrigerate it for at least 30 minutes and up to 8 hours for a more intense soy flavor.) Heat broiler. Transfer the meat to a rimmed baking sheet lined with foil, reserving the marinade in the saucepan. Sprinkle the meat with the pepper. Broil to the desired doneness, about 5 minutes per side for medium-rare. Transfer to a cutting board and let rest for 5 minutes. Meanwhile, place the saucepan containing the marinade over medium-high heat and bring to a boil. Add the scallions, reduce heat, and simmer for 2 minutes. Thinly slice the meat across the grain. To serve, divide the rice among individual bowls and arrange the meat on top. Spoon the scallions and sauce over the meat, and sprinkle with the sesame seeds.

··· Tip

Slice the meat at a slant across the grain to ensure maximum tenderness. This technique works on most relatively inexpensive cuts of steak, including flank, skirt, and top round.

30-minute meals

NOT-SO-SLOPPY JOES

hands-on time: 20 minutes | total time: 30 minutes | makes 4 servings

1 tablespoon olive oil
1 small yellow onion, finely chopped
1 clove garlic, finely chopped
1 red bell pepper, finely chopped
1 pound ground beef
1 6-ounce can tomato paste
1 1/2 teaspoons chili powder
1 teaspoon ground cumin
1/8 teaspoon black pepper
1/8 teaspoon ground cinnamon
1 teaspoon kosher salt
4 hamburger buns, toasted
1/2 cup (2 ounces) grated Cheddar (optional)
1/2 cup sour cream (optional)

Heat the oil in a large saucepan over medium heat. Add the onion, garlic, and bell pepper. Cook until softened, about 3 minutes. Add the beef and cook, crumbling it with a spoon, until no trace of pink remains, about 7 minutes. Spoon off and discard any excess fat. Stir in the tomato paste, chili powder, cumin, black pepper, cinnamon, and salt. Simmer, stirring occasionally, until the sauce thickens slightly, about 12 minutes. Spoon the beef mixture onto the bottom half of each bun and top with the Cheddar and a dollop of the sour cream (if using). Sandwich with the top half of each bun.

and the next time, try...
Trading in the beef for ground turkey or even vegetarian meat crumbles. Given the sauce's piquant flavor, no one will ever taste the difference.

•••Tip
Don't forget to toast the buns. This quick but necessary step ensures that the bread doesn't turn to mush the second the juices hit the roll.

SAUSAGES WITH WARM TOMATOES AND HASH BROWNS

hands-on time: 30 minutes | total time: 30 minutes | makes 4 servings

2 tablespoons olive oil

8 sweet Italian sausage links

4 tablespoons unsalted butter

1½ pounds russet potatoes,
peeled and grated

1 small yellow onion, grated

2 teaspoons kosher salt

1 teaspoon black pepper

¼ cup plus 2 tablespoons chopped
fresh flat-leaf parsley leaves

18 cherry or grape tomatoes
(red, yellow, or orange), halved

Heat the oil in a large skillet over medium heat. Prick the sausages with a fork. Cook, turning occasionally, until browned and cooked through, about 20 minutes. Meanwhile, melt the butter in another large skillet over medium heat. Add the potatoes and onion and cook until softened, about 5 minutes. Season with 1½ teaspoons of the salt, ½ teaspoon of the pepper, and ¼ cup of the parsley. Gently press the potatoes into the bottom of the skillet with a spatula. Cook, without stirring, until a crust forms, about 5 minutes. Then use the spatula to break apart the potatoes, turn the pieces, and press down again. Cook until another crust forms, about 5 minutes. Cover, reduce heat to medium-low, and cook for 10 minutes. Meanwhile, transfer the sausages to a plate and cover with foil to keep warm. Spoon off and discard all but about 2 tablespoons of the fat from the skillet that contained the sausages. Add the tomatoes and the remaining salt, pepper, and parsley. Cook until the tomatoes soften slightly, about 5 minutes. Serve the sausages with the hash browns and tomatoes.

••• Tip

For faster cooking, halve the sausage links lengthwise before adding them to the skillet. (You can also try this speedy technique with hot dogs.)

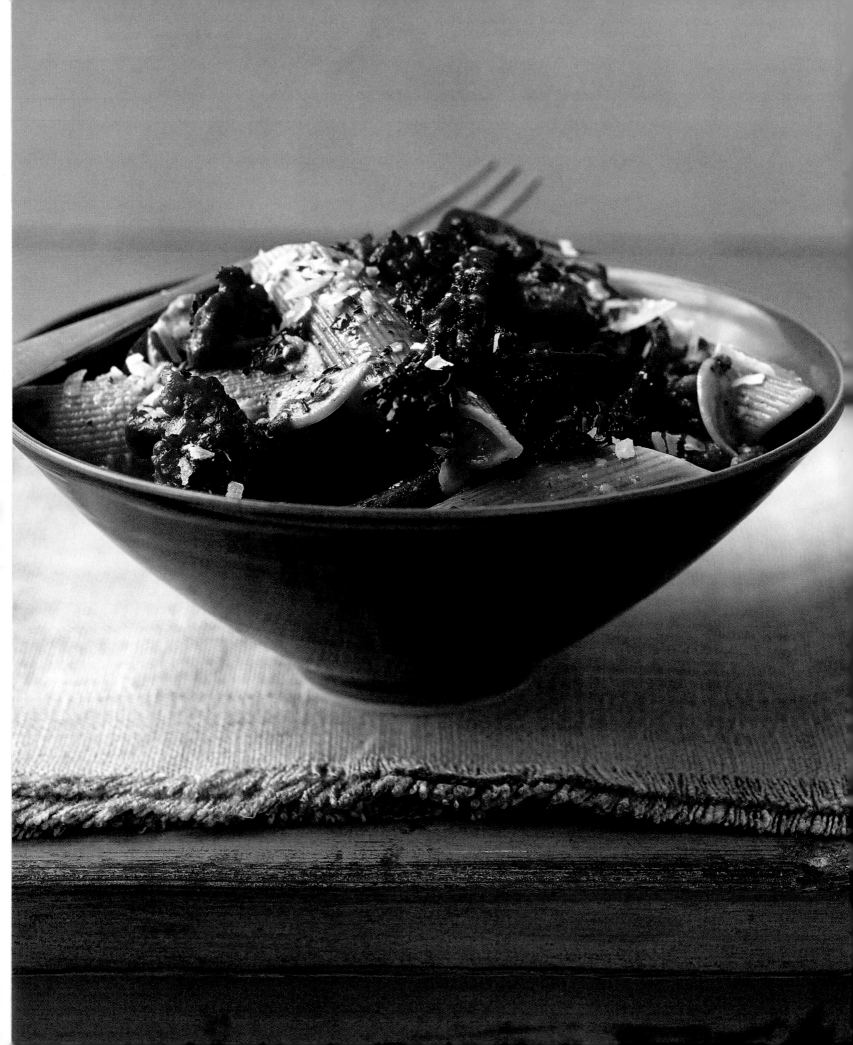

PASTA WITH BROCCOLI RABE AND SAUSAGE

hands-on time: 20 minutes | total time: 30 minutes | makes 4 servings

1 pound dry rigatoni, penne, or ziti

1 tablespoon olive oil

1 pound chicken or pork sausage, casings removed

2 cloves garlic, thinly sliced

1 14.5-ounce can low-sodium chicken broth

1/8 teaspoon red pepper flakes

1 bunch broccoli rabe, trimmed and cut into 1-inch pieces

4 tablespoons unsalted butter

1 1/2 cups (6 ounces) grated Parmesan

1/4 teaspoon kosher salt

1/4 teaspoon black pepper

Cook the pasta according to the package directions. Meanwhile, heat the oil in a large saucepan over medium heat. Add the sausage and cook, crumbling it with a spoon, until no trace of pink remains, about 7 minutes. Spoon off and discard any excess fat. Add the garlic and cook for 1 minute. Add the broth and red pepper flakes and bring to a boil. Add the broccoli rabe, cover, and cook until tender, about 3 minutes. Stir in the butter and Parmesan and cook, uncovered, until the sauce thickens slightly, about 2 minutes. Add the drained pasta, salt, and black pepper and toss to combine. Set aside for a few minutes before serving to allow the pasta to absorb some of the flavorful liquid. To serve, divide the pasta among individual bowls.

and the next time, try...
Using a less pungent green in place of the broccoli rabe. Try broccoli florets to create a milder version or, for a more peppery dish, go with Swiss chard.

•••Tip
Cook pasta in plenty of salted water. The salt will help bring out the natural flavor of the pasta, and the generous amount of water will prevent the noodles from sticking to one another.

30-minute meals

SPICED LAMB CHOPS WITH CHICKPEA SALAD

hands-on time: 20 minutes | total time: 30 minutes | makes 4 servings

1 15-ounce can chickpeas,
  drained and rinsed
4 plum tomatoes, thickly sliced
1 small yellow or red onion,
  sliced into half-moons
3/4 cup fresh flat-leaf parsley leaves,
  roughly chopped
3/4 cup fresh mint leaves, chopped
2 teaspoons white wine vinegar
1 clove garlic, crushed
5 tablespoons olive oil
  Zest of 1 lemon, grated
3 tablespoons fresh lemon juice
1 teaspoon kosher salt
1/2 teaspoon black pepper
1 tablespoon ground cumin
1 tablespoon ground coriander
1 teaspoon paprika
8 lamb loin chops

In a large bowl, combine the chickpeas, tomatoes, onion, parsley, mint, vinegar, garlic, 3 tablespoons of the oil, the lemon zest and juice, 1/2 teaspoon of the salt, and 1/4 teaspoon of the pepper; set aside. In a separate bowl, combine the cumin, coriander, paprika, and the remaining salt and pepper. Lightly coat each of the lamb chops with the spice mixture. Heat 1 tablespoon of the remaining oil in a skillet over medium-high heat. Add half of the lamb chops to the skillet, being careful not to crowd them. Cook to the desired doneness, 2 to 3 minutes per side for medium-rare. Transfer to a plate. Repeat with the remaining oil and lamb chops. Divide the chickpea salad among individual plates and top each salad with 2 lamb chops.

and the next time, try...
Making the salad with canned, drained white beans instead of chickpeas.

••• Tip
Lamb loin chops are exceptionally tender, reasonably priced cuts. Do not confuse them with rib chops, which are daintier and more expensive.

30-minute meals

LEMON-HERB SEAFOOD STIR-FRY

hands-on time: 30 minutes | total time: 30 minutes | makes 4 servings

1/4 cup low-sodium soy sauce

2 1/2 tablespoons fresh lemon juice

2 large cloves garlic, finely chopped

1 1/2 tablespoons sugar

1 1/2 tablespoons chopped fresh basil leaves

1 1/2 tablespoons chopped fresh cilantro leaves

1 pound sea scallops

2 1/2 tablespoons olive oil

1/3 pound sugar snap peas

5 ounces fresh spinach or watercress
  Cooked white rice, preferably jasmine or basmati

In a small bowl, combine the soy sauce, lemon juice, garlic, and sugar, stirring until the sugar dissolves. Add the basil and cilantro; set aside. Rinse the scallops and pat them dry with paper towels. Heat a wok or large skillet over medium-high heat. Add 2 tablespoons of the oil and heat for 30 seconds. Add the scallops. Cook on one side until browned, about 3 minutes. Turn and cook until the scallops are the same color throughout, 1 to 2 minutes more. Transfer to a plate. Wipe out the pan with a paper towel. Add the remaining oil and heat for 30 seconds. Add the peas and 2 tablespoons of water. Cover partially and cook, stirring occasionally, until the peas are bright green, about 1 minute. Add the spinach or watercress and the lemon-herb sauce. When the sauce starts bubbling, add the scallops. Stir-fry until warmed through, about 1 minute. Serve over the rice.

•••Tip

As you heat the oil, keep an eye on the wok. If you see wisps of smoke rising from the pan—a telltale sign the temperature is too high—carefully pour out the oil, wipe out the pan with a paper towel, and start over.

CHAPTER FOUR

no-cook meals

Whether you blame it on an oppressive summer heat wave or on your oppressive work schedule, there are some nights when you simply cannot bear to turn on the stove. But a night without cooking doesn't have to mean a night with takeout. Instead, try your hand at cutting-board cuisine—a far more interesting (and often healthier) alternative. With just a few fresh ingredients, a knife, and—you guessed it—a cutting board, you'll be ready to serve supper without going anywhere near a burner...or a drive-thru.

CANTALOUPE SOUP WITH PROSCIUTTO AND MOZZARELLA SANDWICHES

hands-on time: 25 minutes | total time: 25 minutes | makes 6 to 8 servings

2 baguettes

2 8-ounce balls fresh mozzarella, thickly sliced

1/2 pound prosciutto, thinly sliced

2 tablespoons extra-virgin olive oil

1/4 teaspoon black pepper

2 cantaloupes, chilled

1/2 teaspoon kosher salt

16 fresh mint leaves, chopped if desired

Halve each baguette lengthwise, then cut it crosswise into 3 or 4 portions. Place some of the mozzarella and prosciutto on the bottom half of each portion. Drizzle with the oil and sprinkle with the pepper. Sandwich with the top half of each baguette portion. Transfer to individual plates. Halve each cantaloupe and remove and discard the seeds. Scoop the melon into a blender. Add the salt and puree until smooth. Pour into individual bowls and sprinkle with the mint. Serve alongside the prosciutto and mozzarella sandwiches.

Tip

To select a ripe cantaloupe, look beneath the raised pattern on the melon's rind. The background color should be cream, not green. If you're still uncertain, smell it close to the stem end; it should have a sweet, faintly musty aroma. The ends should also yield slightly to pressure.

no-cook meals

CHICKEN SALAD WITH PEACHES AND BLUE CHEESE

hands-on time: 20 minutes | total time: 20 minutes | makes 6 servings

2 heads romaine lettuce, leaves cut crosswise into 1-inch strips
1 store-bought rotisserie chicken, meat sliced into bite-size pieces
2 peaches, roughly chopped (peel first, if desired)
3/4 cup (3 ounces) crumbled blue cheese
1/2 cup (2 ounces) almonds, roughly chopped
1/4 cup white wine vinegar
1/4 cup extra-virgin olive oil
1 teaspoon kosher salt
1/4 teaspoon black pepper

Arrange the lettuce, chicken, peaches, cheese, and almonds on a platter or on individual plates. Whisk together the vinegar, oil, salt, and pepper in a small bowl. Drizzle the vinaigrette over the salad.

and the next time, try...
Customizing the salad based on the season—or the contents of your refrigerator:
• Use thinly sliced pears or halved red grapes in place of the peaches.
• Replace the romaine lettuce with spinach, arugula, or watercress.
• Swap goat cheese for the blue.
• Go with walnuts instead of the almonds.

•••Tip
The best blue cheeses for salads are dry and crumbly in texture and not overwhelmingly pungent. Try a Roquefort or a Maytag blue.

SMOKED SALMON WITH CUCUMBER AND WATERCRESS

hands-on time: 15 minutes | total time: 20 minutes | makes 6 servings

2 bunches watercress, ends
  trimmed
1 pound smoked salmon, thinly
  sliced
4 teaspoons prepared horseradish
4 teaspoons coarse-grain
  mustard
1/2 cup sour cream
1/4 cup fresh lemon juice
1/2 teaspoon kosher salt
1/4 teaspoon black pepper
2 small cucumbers
  Bagel chips, crackers, or thinly
  sliced baguette, toasted

Separate the watercress into single sprigs. Arrange the watercress and salmon on a platter or on individual plates. In a bowl, whisk together the horseradish, mustard, sour cream, lemon juice, salt, and pepper until smooth. Transfer half the dressing to a small serving bowl; set aside. Halve each cucumber lengthwise and thinly slice. Add the cucumbers to the remaining dressing and toss to coat. Divide the cucumber mixture among the plates. Serve with the bagel chips, crackers, or toasted bread and the reserved dressing.

···Tip
Seeding a cucumber that is destined for a salad isn't required, but it will make the salad less watery. Just halve the cucumber lengthwise, then use a spoon to scoop out and discard the seeds.

no-cook meals

SWEET PEA AND MINT SOUP

hands-on time: 15 minutes | total time: 15 minutes | makes 4 servings

2 10-ounce packages (4 cups)
   frozen peas, thawed slightly
3/4 cup fresh mint leaves
4 scallions, roughly chopped
3 cups low-sodium chicken
   or vegetable broth
1 teaspoon kosher salt
1 teaspoon sugar

Place all the ingredients in a blender. Puree until smooth, at least 1 minute. To serve, pour into individual bowls.

and the next time, try...
Embellishing this delicate recipe with a few simple touches:
• Strain the soup for a silky smooth texture.
• Add a dollop of crème fraîche, sour cream, or plain yogurt.
• Sprinkle with torn fresh mint leaves.

••• Tip
Keep a few bags of frozen peas around at all times. Not only do the peas retain a surprisingly fresh, springlike flavor when frozen but the bags make great impromptu ice packs.

TUNA IN A TOMATO

hands-on time: 20 minutes | total time: 20 minutes | makes 6 servings

6 large tomatoes

3 6-ounce cans tuna, drained

3 tablespoons capers, roughly
  chopped

1 cup fresh flat-leaf parsley
leaves, roughly chopped

  Zest of 1 lemon

1/4 cup fresh lemon juice

1 tablespoon extra-virgin olive oil

1/4 teaspoon black pepper

With a paring knife, cut out and discard the stem of each tomato. Using a spoon, hollow out the tomatoes, leaving each with a 1/4-inch shell, and transfer the pulp to a medium bowl. Add the remaining ingredients to the tomato pulp and toss gently. Spoon the mixture back into the tomatoes and serve.

and the next time, try...

Introducing new flavors and textures to the filling:

• Use basil in place of parsley.

• Substitute chopped olives for capers.

• Add finely chopped red onion or scallions.

• Opt for equal amounts of mayonnaise and sour cream in place of the olive oil.

• Stir in a couple of spoonfuls of cooked rice.

•••Tip

In the summer, make this recipe with heirloom tomatoes, which come in vibrant colors. Yellow and orange heirlooms tend to be less acidic than red ones; purple heirlooms are often earthier and more intense in flavor.

no-cook meals

GREEK SALAD

hands-on time: 15 minutes | total time: 15 minutes | makes 4 to 6 servings

8 tablespoons extra-virgin olive oil

1 cup fresh basil leaves

1/4 teaspoon kosher salt

8 ounces Feta, thickly sliced

1 medium cucumber, chopped
  (peel first, if desired)

8 ounces cherry or grape
  tomatoes, halved

3/4 cup kalamata olives, pitted
  if desired

1 12-ounce jar pepperoncini,
  drained

2 14-ounce jars dolmades (optional)

1/4 teaspoon black pepper

1 lemon, cut into wedges

In a blender or food processor, puree the oil, basil, and salt; set aside. Arrange the Feta, cucumber, tomatoes, olives, pepperoncini, and dolmades (if using) on a platter or on individual plates. Drizzle with the basil oil and sprinkle with the pepper. Serve with the lemon wedges on the side.

and the next time, try...
Breathing new life into the leftovers by chopping them and tossing with day-old bread or freshly cooked pasta. Sprinkle with basil leaves, if you have any extra lying around.

•••Tip
Dolmades—essentially grape leaves stuffed with rice—can be found at many Greek and Italian delis, as well as in the olive aisle in supermarkets. Pepperoncini (mildly hot pickled peppers) are available in Italian delis or near the pickles in some supermarkets.

PAN BAGNAT

hands-on time: 20 minutes | total time: 20 minutes | makes 3 to 4 servings

1 baguette
2 6-ounce cans tuna, drained
1/2 teaspoon kosher salt
1/4 teaspoon black pepper
2 tablespoons fresh lemon juice
3 tablespoons extra-virgin olive oil
1 head green leaf or Boston lettuce
2 plum tomatoes, sliced crosswise
1/2 small red onion, thinly sliced
1/3 cup kalamata olives,
    pitted and roughly chopped
1/3 cup fresh basil leaves
3 tablespoons capers, roughly
    chopped (optional)

Halve the baguette lengthwise, then cut it crosswise into 3 or 4 portions. Remove some of the light, fluffy bread from the center and discard or reserve for another use (such as bread crumbs). In a medium bowl, combine the tuna, salt, pepper, lemon juice, and 1 tablespoon of the oil. Place a few lettuce leaves on both halves of each baguette portion. Top the bottom halves with the tuna mixture, tomatoes, onion, olives, basil, and capers (if using). Drizzle with the remaining oil. Sandwich with the top half of each baguette portion and press gently but firmly.

and the next time, try...
Giving this French sandwich an international flavor by replacing the baguette with whole-grain bread, pita, or whatever happens to be sitting on the counter (pumpernickel, anyone?).

•••Tip
Pit the olives by placing them on a cutting board and pressing on them with the flat side of a chef's knife. The pits should pop right out; if they're being stubborn, pinch each olive to coax the pit out.

no-cook meals

PANZANELLA

hands-on time: 25 minutes | total time: 25 minutes | makes 8 servings

1 loaf day-old whole-wheat or
   white bread, preferably unsliced
6 large tomatoes, cut into wedges
1 large red onion, thinly sliced
1/4 cup kalamata olives, pitted and
   roughly chopped if desired
1/2 cup fresh basil leaves, chopped
1/2 cup extra-virgin olive oil
1/4 cup red wine vinegar
1/4 cup fresh lemon juice
1/2 teaspoon kosher salt
1/4 cup chopped fresh flat-leaf
   parsley leaves (optional)
1/2 cup (2 ounces) shaved Parmesan

Remove and discard the crust from the bread, if desired. Tear or cut the bread into 1-inch pieces; you will need about 5 cups total. Place the bread in a large bowl along with the tomatoes, onion, olives, and basil. In a separate bowl, whisk together the oil, vinegar, lemon juice, salt, and parsley (if using). Drizzle the vinaigrette over the bread mixture and toss. To serve, transfer to individual plates and scatter the Parmesan over the top.

and the next time, try…
Preparing panzanella the truly Italian—if slightly soggy—way. Set it aside at room temperature for about an hour before serving to allow the bread to absorb the flavorful tomato juices and vinaigrette.

••• Tip
To shave Parmesan, pull a vegetable peeler lightly but firmly across the surface of the cheese. It will fall away in ribbons.

GAZPACHO

hands-on time: 30 minutes | total time: 2 hours, 30 minutes (includes chilling) | makes 8 servings

3 small fennel bulbs, roughly chopped

4 celery stalks, roughly chopped

1 bunch scallions, roughly chopped

1 medium sweet onion, roughly chopped

2 small cloves garlic, chopped

3 red bell peppers, roughly chopped

2 large tomatoes, diced, or one 14.5-ounce can diced tomatoes, undrained

1/2 cup extra-virgin olive oil

1 tablespoon kosher salt

1/2 teaspoon black pepper

1 32-ounce container (4 cups) tomato or vegetable juice

1/3 cup fresh lemon juice

Celery leaves (optional)

Fresh dill (optional)

Place the fennel, celery stalks, scallions, onion, garlic, and bell peppers in the bowl of a food processor. Pulse until the mixture is finely chopped and combined but not pureed. Pour the mixture into a large glass or plastic bowl. Stir in the tomatoes with their juices, oil, salt, black pepper, tomato or vegetable juice, and lemon juice. Cover and refrigerate for at least 2 hours. To serve, sprinkle with the celery leaves, dill, or both (if using).

and the next time, try...

Personalizing the recipe:

• Puree the soup for a smoother texture.

• For a touch of heat, stir in 1 teaspoon hot sauce.

• Trade in the celery leaves or dill for fresh basil.

···Tip

Because the vegetables are destined for the food processor, there's no need to spend time dicing them precisely. Just give them a quick, rough chop.

no-cook meals

SHRIMP, WATERMELON, AND AVOCADO SALAD

hands-on time: 20 minutes | total time: 30 minutes | makes 6 servings

1 1-pound package frozen cooked
  shrimp, thawed
4 cups watermelon, seeded and
  roughly chopped
1 medium red onion, thinly sliced
1/2 cup fresh cilantro leaves
2 jalapeños, seeded and finely
  chopped
2 avocados, roughly chopped
  Juice of 1 lime
1 teaspoon honey
3 tablespoons extra-virgin olive oil
3/4 teaspoon kosher salt
1/4 teaspoon black pepper

Place the shrimp, watermelon, onion, cilantro, jalapeños, and avocados in a large bowl. In a separate bowl, whisk together the lime juice, honey, oil, salt, and pepper. Pour the vinaigrette over the salad and toss gently. Set aside for 10 minutes before serving to allow the flavors to meld.

and the next time, try...
Tossing together a winterized version of this kaleidoscopic summery salad. Swap in sections of pink grapefruit for the watermelon cubes, and try mint in place of the cilantro.

•••Tip
Cut down on prep time (not to mention refrigerator-shelf space) by using a "personal-size" watermelon (available in most supermarkets). It weighs only 4 to 6 pounds and contains few, if any, seeds.

CHAPTER FIVE

freezer meals

The humble frozen dinner holds an esteemed position in the harried cook's kitchen. It's no mystery why: When you have to work late but your kids have to eat early, your best—some might say *only*—option is to rely on a heat-and-serve meal. To that end, the freezer-friendly recipes here are custom-designed for you to make ahead of time and use whenever. So your family can sit down to a dinner that's stick-a-fork-in-it done—whether or not you're there to join them. Talk about frozen assets.

PASTA WITH BOLOGNESE SAUCE

hands-on time: 20 minutes | total time: 1 hour, 25 minutes | makes 4 to 6 servings

1 tablespoon olive oil

1 large yellow onion, finely chopped

3 celery stalks, finely chopped

1 carrot, finely chopped

4 cloves garlic, finely chopped

1/4 pound pancetta, finely chopped

1 1/2 pounds ground beef

1 cup dry white wine

1 cup whole milk

1 6-ounce can tomato paste

1 14.5-ounce can diced tomatoes, undrained

1/4 teaspoon red pepper flakes

2 tablespoons chopped fresh oregano or 1 1/2 teaspoons dried oregano

1/2 cup fresh flat-leaf parsley leaves, chopped

2 1/2 teaspoons kosher salt

1/4 teaspoon black pepper

1/8 teaspoon grated nutmeg

1 pound dry fettuccine
Grated Parmesan

Heat the oil in a Dutch oven or large saucepan over medium heat. Add the onion and cook for 3 minutes. Add the celery, carrot, and garlic and cook for 5 minutes. Add the pancetta and cook for 5 minutes. Add the beef and cook, crumbling it with a spoon, until no trace of pink remains, about 7 minutes. Spoon off and discard any excess fat. Add the wine, milk, tomato paste, tomatoes, red pepper flakes, oregano, parsley, salt, black pepper, and nutmeg and bring to a simmer. Cover partially, reduce heat, and simmer for 45 minutes. Meanwhile, cook the pasta according to the package directions. Drain and transfer to individual bowls. Top with the sauce and Parmesan.

to freeze...

Omit the pasta and the Parmesan. Let the sauce cool, then ladle it into resealable freezer bags. Store for up to 3 months.

to reheat...

Thaw the sauce overnight in the refrigerator or thaw partially in the microwave. Warm in a covered saucepan over medium-low heat for 20 minutes. Meanwhile, cook the pasta. Spoon the sauce over it and sprinkle with the Parmesan.

••• Tip

Minimize the amount of freezer space taken up by soups, stews, or sauces by freezing them into flat packets. Fill a resealable plastic bag halfway, removing as much air as possible before sealing it. Lay the bag flat on a baking sheet and freeze until solid. Then stand the packet on its side.

freezer meals

BUTTERNUT SQUASH SOUP

hands-on time: 25 minutes | total time: 2 hours | makes 6 to 8 servings

1 3-pound butternut squash
3 tablespoons olive oil
3 teaspoons kosher salt
1/8 teaspoon black pepper
1 tablespoon unsalted butter
1 large yellow onion, chopped
3 celery stalks, chopped
1 tablespoon chopped fresh
   sage leaves
1 32-ounce container
   low-sodium chicken broth

Heat oven to 400° F. Peel and seed the squash. Cut it into 1-inch cubes and place them on a rimmed baking sheet. Drizzle with 2 tablespoons of the oil, 2 teaspoons of the salt, and the pepper and toss to coat. Spread in a single layer and roast for 15 minutes. Turn and continue to roast until softened, about 15 minutes more. Meanwhile, heat the butter and the remaining oil in a stockpot over medium heat. Add the onion, celery, and sage and cook until softened, about 7 minutes. Add the broth, 2 cups of water, the remaining salt, and the squash and bring to a boil. Reduce heat and simmer for 30 minutes. Remove from heat. Let cool for 10 minutes. Working in batches, transfer the soup to a blender and puree until smooth. Return to the pot and warm over medium-low heat.

to freeze...
Let the soup cool, then ladle it into resealable freezer bags. Store for up to 3 months.

to reheat...
Thaw overnight in the refrigerator or thaw partially in the microwave. Warm in a covered saucepan over medium-low heat for 20 minutes.

···Tip
Roasting the squash before you add it to the soup results in a rich, caramelized flavor. But if you don't have the time, skip this step. Want to save a few more minutes? Look for peeled, cubed butternut squash in the produce section or frozen-vegetable aisle of your supermarket.

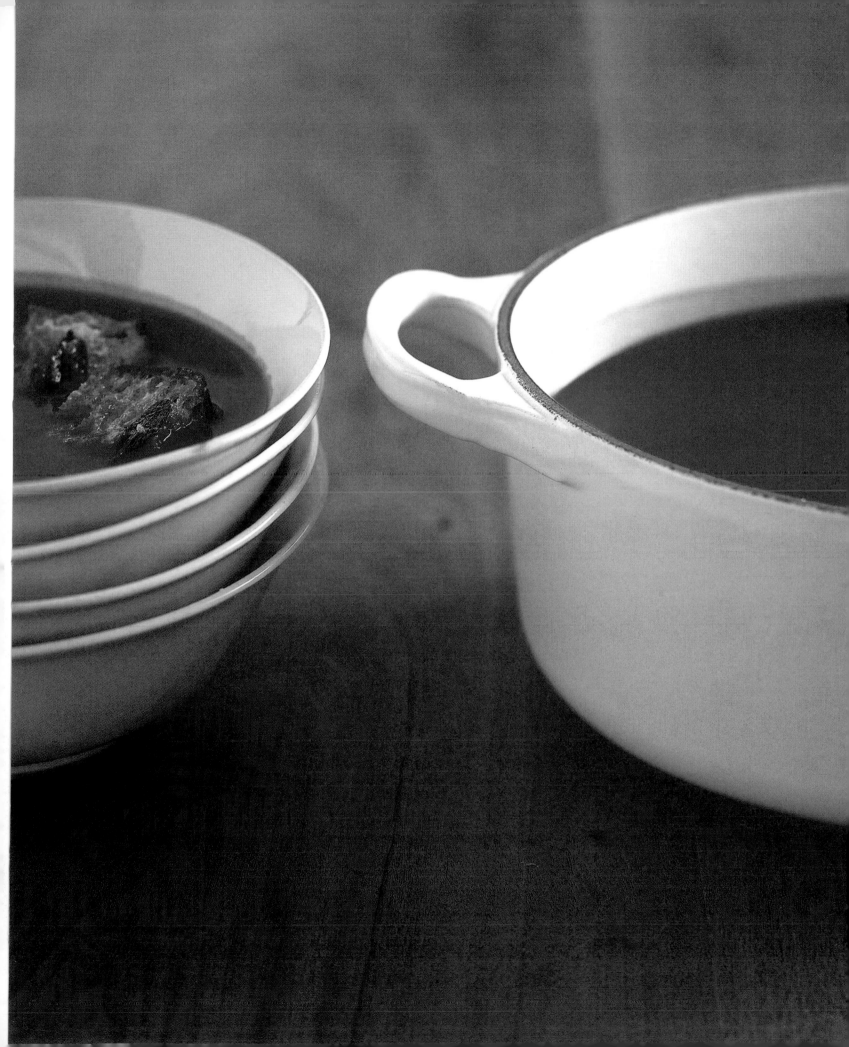

freezer meals

SMOKY SPLIT-PEA SOUP

hands-on time: 15 minutes | total time: 4 hours, 25 minutes | makes 4 to 6 servings

2 ham hocks (about 1½ pounds total)
1 pound green split peas
2 carrots, chopped
2 celery stalks, chopped
1 large yellow onion, chopped
2 cloves garlic, finely chopped
2 32-ounce containers low-sodium chicken broth
1 bay leaf
1 tablespoon fresh thyme leaves or 1 teaspoon dried thyme

Rinse the ham hocks. Place them in a stockpot or Dutch oven along with the remaining ingredients. Bring to a boil. Reduce heat to medium-low, cover, and cook for 3½ to 4 hours. Remove and discard the bay leaf. Transfer the ham hocks to a plate and let cool. When the meat is cool enough to handle, chop or shred it and return it to the soup. Ladle the soup into individual bowls.

to freeze...

Let the soup cool, then ladle it into resealable freezer bags. Store for up to 3 months.

to reheat...

Thaw overnight in the refrigerator or thaw partially in the microwave. Warm the soup in a covered saucepan over medium-low heat for 15 minutes. If the soup seems too thick, stir in up to 1 cup of water to attain the desired consistency.

···Tip
Look for ham hocks in the meat case, near the bacon. If you can't find them, substitute ½ pound of bacon, diced and fried until brown but not crisp, and add an extra pinch of salt.

freezer meals

MUSHROOM BARLEY SOUP

hands-on time: 35 minutes | total time: 45 minutes | makes 4 to 6 servings

1 cup barley
1 1/2 tablespoons olive oil
2 medium yellow onions, chopped
1/2 teaspoon kosher salt
1/4 teaspoon black pepper
1 carrot, chopped
2 celery stalks, chopped
20 ounces button mushrooms, stems trimmed, caps thinly sliced
3 14.5-ounce cans low-sodium chicken or vegetable broth
2 bay leaves
8 sprigs fresh thyme
Sourdough or country bread, toasted (optional)

Bring the barley and 4 cups of water to a boil in a medium saucepan. Reduce heat, cover, and simmer until tender, 30 to 40 minutes. Meanwhile, heat the oil in a large pot over medium-low heat. Add the onions, salt, and pepper. Cook for 5 minutes. Add the carrot and celery and cook for 6 minutes more. Add the mushrooms, increase heat to medium-high, and cook until they release their juices, about 3 minutes. Add the broth, bay leaves, and thyme and simmer for 10 minutes. Stir in the cooked barley and cook for 5 minutes more. Remove and discard the bay leaves and thyme sprigs. Ladle into individual bowls and serve with the toasted bread, if desired.

to freeze...
Let the soup cool, then ladle it into resealable freezer bags. Store for up to 3 months.

to reheat...
Thaw overnight in the refrigerator or thaw partially in the microwave. Warm in a covered saucepan over medium-low heat for 20 minutes. Serve with the toasted bread, if desired.

···•Tip
If you're finding it difficult to extricate food that has been frozen in a plastic bag, use scissors to cut the bag, then simply peel the plastic away.

LASAGNA-STYLE BAKED ZITI

hands-on time: 20 minutes | total time: 45 minutes | makes 4 to 6 servings

1 pound dry ziti
1 tablespoon olive oil
1 large yellow onion, chopped
3/4 teaspoon kosher salt
1/4 teaspoon black pepper
1 pound ground beef
3 cloves garlic, finely chopped
1/2 cup chopped fresh oregano
or 1 1/2 tablespoons dried
oregano (optional)
1 24- to 26-ounce jar pasta sauce
1 15-ounce container ricotta
1 10-ounce box frozen spinach,
thawed and squeezed to
remove excess moisture
1/2 cup (2 ounces) grated
Parmesan
1 cup (4 ounces) shredded
mozzarella

Heat oven to 400° F. Cook the ziti according to the package directions. Meanwhile, heat the oil in a large pot over medium heat. Add the onion, salt, and pepper and cook for 5 minutes. Add the beef and cook, crumbling it with a spoon, until no trace of pink remains, about 7 minutes. Spoon off and discard any excess fat. Add the garlic and oregano (if using) and cook for 2 minutes. Add the pasta sauce and cook for 3 minutes. Remove from heat. Add the drained ziti to the pot and toss. Add the ricotta, spinach, and 1/4 cup of the Parmesan and toss again. Spread the mixture into a 9-by-13-inch baking dish. Sprinkle with the mozzarella and the remaining Parmesan. Bake until the mozzarella melts, about 15 minutes.

to freeze...
Assemble—but do not bake—the casserole. Cover tightly with two layers of aluminum foil. Store for up to 3 months.

to reheat...
Thaw overnight in the refrigerator or thaw partially in the microwave. Cover and heat in a 350° F oven for 1 hour. Uncover and heat until the mozzarella melts, about 10 minutes more.

••• Tip

Don't allow your baking dish to be taken hostage by a frozen casserole. Before placing food in the dish, line it with several layers of foil. After freezing, lift the foil and food from the dish and wrap it tightly in plastic wrap. When you are ready to thaw the food, remove the plastic wrap and foil and return the icy block to its dish.

freezer meals

PASTA AND BEANS

hands-on time: 15 minutes | total time: 2 hours (includes soaking) | makes 6 to 8 servings

1 16-ounce bag dried cannellini
   or navy beans
1 large yellow onion, finely
   chopped
2 celery stalks, finely chopped
5 cloves garlic, finely chopped
1 tablespoon chopped fresh sage
   leaves or 1 teaspoon dried sage
1 tablespoon finely chopped
   fresh rosemary or 1 teaspoon
   dried rosemary
1 14.5-ounce can low-sodium
   chicken broth
1 14.5-ounce can diced tomatoes,
   undrained
1 cup dry small pasta, such as
   ditalini or tubettini
1 tablespoon kosher salt
1 tablespoon black pepper
1/4 teaspoon red pepper flakes
1 tablespoon extra-virgin olive oil
   Shaved Parmesan

Bring the beans and 6 cups of water to a boil in a Dutch oven or stockpot. Cook, stirring occasionally, for 5 minutes. Remove from heat, cover, and let soak for 45 minutes. Drain the beans and return them to the pot. Add the onion, celery, garlic, sage, rosemary, broth, and 10 cups of water. Bring to a boil. Reduce heat to a simmer. Cook, stirring occasionally, until the beans are tender, 30 to 40 minutes. Add the tomatoes and cook for 10 minutes. Add the pasta, salt, black pepper, and red pepper flakes. Cook until the pasta is al dente, 5 to 7 minutes. Ladle the soup into bowls, drizzle with the oil, and sprinkle with the Parmesan.

to freeze...
Omit the pasta, oil, and Parmesan. Let the soup cool, then ladle it into resealable freezer bags. Store for up to 3 months.

to reheat...
Thaw the soup overnight in the refrigerator. Warm in a covered saucepan over medium-low heat for 20 minutes. Uncover and bring to a simmer. Add the pasta and cook for 5 to 7 minutes more. Drizzle with the oil and sprinkle with the Parmesan.

•••Tip
Small pasta shapes are ideal for soup because they cook quickly and don't overwhelm the other ingredients. If you can't find them in your supermarket, substitute an equal amount of spaghetti broken into small pieces.

CHEESY VEGETABLE PASTA

hands-on time: 25 minutes | total time: 1 hour, 20 minutes | makes 4 servings

1/2 pound dry ziti or penne
1 tablespoon balsamic vinegar
3/4 teaspoon kosher salt
1/4 cup olive oil
2 medium zucchini, halved
  lengthwise
2 medium eggplants, halved
  lengthwise
1/2 large yellow onion, quartered
2 large cloves garlic,
  finely chopped
1 1/2 teaspoons fresh oregano or
  1/2 teaspoon dried oregano
4 plum tomatoes, chopped
1 cup pasta sauce
3/4 cup (3 ounces) crumbled Feta
1/4 teaspoon black pepper
1/2 teaspoon red pepper flakes
2 cups (8 ounces) shredded
  mozzarella

Cook the pasta according to the package directions. Meanwhile, whisk together the vinegar, 1/2 teaspoon of the salt, and 1 tablespoon of the oil in a small bowl. Place the zucchini, eggplants, and onion on a baking sheet. Brush with the vinaigrette. Heat broiler on high. Broil until tender, 8 minutes per side. Heat oven to 350° F. Chop the roasted vegetables. Place a large pot over low heat. Add the garlic and the remaining oil and cook for 3 minutes. Add the drained pasta, vegetables, oregano, tomatoes, pasta sauce, Feta, black pepper, red pepper flakes, and the remaining salt and toss. Transfer to a 9-by-13-inch baking dish. Sprinkle with the mozzarella. Cover and bake for 30 minutes. Uncover and bake for 20 minutes more.

to freeze...
Assemble—but do not bake—the casserole. Cover tightly with two layers of aluminum foil. Store for up to 3 months.

to reheat...
Thaw overnight in the refrigerator or thaw partially in the microwave. Cover and heat in a 350° F oven for 30 minutes. Uncover and heat for 10 minutes more.

•••Tip
To make individual servings, freeze the pasta in ramekins or small ovenproof bowls. Cover and heat for 20 minutes, then uncover and heat for 10 minutes more.

freezer meals

CLASSIC BEEF STEW

hands-on time: 35 minutes | total time: 4 hours, 30 minutes | makes 8 to 10 servings

4 pounds bottom round, trimmed
and cut into 2-inch pieces, or
4 pounds precut stew meat

1 cup all-purpose flour

1/3 cup olive oil

2 large yellow onions, chopped

1 6-ounce can tomato paste

1 cup dry red wine

1 pound Yukon gold potatoes,
cut into 2-inch pieces (peel
first, if desired)

8 ounces baby-cut carrots

1 14.5-ounce can beef broth

1 tablespoon kosher salt

1 tablespoon fresh thyme
leaves or 1 teaspoon
dried thyme

1 bay leaf

1 cup frozen peas, thawed

Heat oven to 350° F. Lightly coat the beef in the flour. Heat 3 tablespoons of the oil in a Dutch oven over medium-high heat. Add some of the beef to the pot, being careful not to crowd the pieces. Cook until browned, about 7 minutes per side. Transfer to a plate; set aside. Repeat with the remaining oil and beef. Reduce heat to medium, add the onions, and cook for 10 minutes. Add the tomato paste and stir. Add the wine and cook, stirring to scrape up any browned bits, for 1 minute. Add the beef, potatoes, carrots, broth, salt, thyme, and bay leaf. Cover and bring to a boil. Transfer to oven. Cook until the beef is tender, 2 to 2 1/2 hours. Remove and discard the bay leaf. Add the peas and cook over medium-high heat for 3 minutes. Ladle into individual bowls.

to freeze...
Omit the peas. Let the stew cool, then ladle it into resealable freezer bags. Store for up to 3 months.

to reheat...
Thaw the stew overnight in the refrigerator or thaw partially in the microwave. Warm in a covered saucepan over medium-low heat for about 20 minutes, adding the peas during the last 5 minutes.

•••Tip
For a leaner dish, refrigerate the stew overnight before serving or freezing. The fat will rise to the surface and solidify, making it easy to skim and discard.

TURKEY NOODLE SOUP

hands-on time: 25 minutes | total time: 3 hours, 45 minutes | makes 6 servings

1 carcass from a 12- to 14-
pound turkey

1 large yellow onion, quartered

2 teaspoons kosher salt

6 whole black peppercorns

2 sprigs fresh tarragon,
plus 2 tablespoons chopped
tarragon leaves

5 carrots, peeled

5 celery stalks

1 handful celery leaves, chopped
(optional)

8 ounces wide egg noodles

3 cups cooked turkey, cut into
1-inch chunks

1/2 teaspoon black pepper

Place the turkey carcass, onion, salt, peppercorns, and tarragon sprigs in a large pot. Halve 3 of the carrots and 3 of the celery stalks and add them to the pot. Add enough water to cover (about 14 cups). Bring to a boil. Reduce heat, cover partially, and simmer for 1½ hours. Uncover and simmer for 1 to 1½ more hours. Strain the stock, discarding the solids, then return it to the pot. Chop the remaining carrots and celery. Add them to the pot with the celery leaves (if using). Bring to a boil. Add the noodles and cook for 6 minutes. Reduce heat, add the chopped tarragon leaves and turkey meat, and simmer for 5 minutes. Add the pepper and ladle into individual bowls.

to freeze...
Omit the egg noodles. Let the soup cool, then ladle it into resealable plastic freezer bags. Store for up to 3 months.

to reheat...
Thaw the soup overnight in the refrigerator or thaw partially in the microwave. Warm in a covered saucepan over medium-low heat for 20 minutes. Uncover and bring to a simmer. Add the egg noodles and cook for 11 minutes more.

···Tip
When chopping vegetables for your Thanksgiving meal, chop a few extra, place them in plastic bags, and refrigerate them. That way your prep work will be nearly nil when it comes time to make the soup with that leftover turkey.

CHAPTER SIX

shortcut meals

Generally speaking, cheating (on tests, at Scrabble) is wrong. But cheating in the kitchen? That's another story altogether. When you need to put dinner on the table pronto, it's perfectly acceptable to enlist convenience foods like rotisserie chicken, jarred pasta sauce, or even frozen toaster waffles as accomplices—if it means you can skip a step (or ten) in the process. To cover your tracks, all you have to do is add a few other ingredients. And if a trace of guilt still lingers, take comfort: The resulting dishes taste just like homemade, so there's no penalty if you get caught.

CHICKEN POTPIE

hands-on time: 35 minutes | total time: 1 hour, 35 minutes | makes 6 servings

1 stick unsalted butter

5 tablespoons all-purpose flour, plus more for rolling the crust

4 cups low-sodium chicken broth

1 large yellow onion, chopped

2 tablespoons fresh thyme leaves or 2 teaspoons dried thyme

4 carrots, chopped

1 10-ounce package button mushrooms, stems trimmed and caps quartered

1 1/2 teaspoons kosher salt

3/4 teaspoon black pepper

1 store-bought rotisserie chicken, meat shredded

1 10-ounce package frozen peas

1 store-bought piecrust

Heat oven to 425° F. Melt 5 tablespoons of the butter in a medium saucepan over medium heat. Whisking constantly, slowly add the flour and cook for 3 minutes. Still whisking, slowly add the broth. Bring to a boil. Reduce heat and simmer until thickened slightly, about 5 minutes. Remove from heat. Melt 2 tablespoons of the remaining butter in a skillet over medium heat. Add the onion and cook until softened, about 7 minutes. Add the thyme and carrots and cook for 5 minutes more. Transfer to a 9-by-13-inch baking dish. Melt the remaining butter in the skillet over medium-high heat. Add the mushrooms and cook for 2 minutes. Reduce heat, season with 1/2 teaspoon of the salt and 1/4 teaspoon of the pepper, and simmer until the liquid evaporates, about 3 minutes. Add the mushrooms to the dish along with the chicken, peas, the reserved sauce, and the remaining salt and pepper and toss. Roll out the piecrust on a floured surface until it is slightly larger than the dish. Lay it on top and tuck under any dough that hangs over the edges. Cut two 2-inch slits in the crust. Bake until the crust is golden brown, about 20 minutes. Reduce heat to 350° F and bake until the filling starts to bubble, 25 minutes more.

•••Tip

To cut down on last-minute prep, assemble this dish early in the day and refrigerate it, then bake it just before serving.

shortcut meals

SHRIMP FRA DIAVOLO

hands-on time: 5 minutes | total time: 20 minutes | makes 4 servings

1 pound dry spaghetti, fettuccine,
  or linguine
1 1-pound bag frozen uncooked
  shrimp, thawed
2 tablespoons olive oil
1 24- to 26-ounce jar pasta sauce
1/2 to 1 teaspoon red pepper flakes
  or hot sauce

Cook the pasta according to the package directions. Meanwhile, rinse the shrimp and pat them
dry with paper towels. Heat the oil in a large skillet over medium-high heat. Add the shrimp and
cook, turning once, until pink and cooked through,
about 4 minutes total. Transfer to a plate. Add the
pasta sauce to the skillet and cook until heated
through. Drain the pasta and return it to the pot.
Add the pasta sauce, shrimp, and pepper flakes or
hot sauce to the pot and toss. Place over low heat
until warmed through, about 1 minute.

and the next time, try...
Varying the flavor with a few kitchen staples:
• Sauté some garlic or onions, or both, in the oil
  before adding the shrimp.
• Stir in a pinch of grated orange zest and
  crushed fennel seeds when you heat the sauce.
• Drop in a handful of chopped green or black
  olives before tossing the pasta.

•••Tip
**Defrost shrimp on the
double by putting them
in a colander and placing
it in the sink under cool
running water for a few
minutes.**

ANTIPASTO PLATE

hands-on time: 15 minutes | total time: 15 minutes | makes 6 servings

1 pound fresh mozzarella bocconcini or two 8-ounce balls fresh mozzarella

1 6-ounce package thinly sliced salami

2 4-ounce packages bresaola

12 ounces Parmesan

2 5-ounce bags arugula

1 12- to 16-ounce jar roasted red peppers, drained and roughly chopped

1 12-ounce jar giardiniera, drained (optional)

1/2 cup extra-virgin olive oil

3 tablespoons red wine vinegar

1/4 teaspoon kosher salt

1/4 teaspoon black pepper

Cut the mozzarella, salami, and bresaola into 1-inch pieces. Crumble the Parmesan into small chunks. Place 1 large handful of the arugula on each plate. Arrange some of the mozzarella, salami, bresaola, Parmesan, roasted peppers, and giardiniera (if using) on top. Drizzle first with the oil and then with the vinegar. Season with the salt and pepper to taste. Toss gently.

and the next time, try...

Using any or all of the colorful items you find in your local Italian deli: prosciutto, Pecorino, olives, marinated artichokes or mushrooms, caper berries, soppressata, pepperoncini...

•••Tip

Giardiniera are pickled vegetables. You can find them next to the pickles and olives in supermarkets and specialty stores. Bocconcini, small balls of fresh mozzarella, are available at some specialty cheese counters. Bresaola is thinly sliced, salted, air-dried aged beef and is sold in Italian delis and specialty stores.

shortcut meals

INSIDE-OUT SPRING ROLLS

hands-on time: 15 minutes | total time: 15 minutes | makes 4 servings

1 16-ounce bag frozen pot stickers
1 tablespoon olive or peanut oil
1 carrot, thinly sliced on the
  diagonal
1 small head Napa cabbage,
  thinly sliced
2 tablespoons low-sodium
  soy sauce
1/4 cup salted peanuts

Fry the pot stickers according to the package directions. Meanwhile, heat the oil in a nonstick skillet over medium-high heat. Add the carrot and cabbage and toss to coat. Add the soy sauce and cook for 2 to 3 minutes. To serve, transfer the vegetables to individual bowls, top with the pot stickers, and sprinkle with the peanuts.

and the next time, try...
Making your life even easier by substituting 3 cups of packaged slaw mix (found in the produce section of most supermarkets) for the sliced carrot and cabbage.

···•Tip
Napa cabbage (also known as Chinese cabbage) has thinner, more crinkly leaves than standard green cabbage and is much milder in flavor. But if you can't find Napa cabbage at your supermarket, it's perfectly fine to use green cabbage in its place.

LAST-MINUTE LASAGNA

hands-on time: 10 minutes | total time: 45 minutes | makes 6 servings

1 24- to 26-ounce jar pasta sauce
2 16- to 18-ounce bags frozen large
  cheese ravioli, unthawed
1 10-ounce box frozen chopped
  spinach, thawed and squeezed
  to remove excess water
1 8-ounce bag shredded mozzarella
1/2 cup (2 ounces) grated Parmesan

Heat oven to 350° F. Spoon 1/3 of the pasta sauce into a 9-by-13-inch baking dish. Place half of the ravioli on top of the sauce in a single layer. Sprinkle with the spinach and half of the mozzarella. Layer on the remaining ravioli (you may not need all of them). Top with the remaining sauce and mozzarella and the Parmesan. Cover with foil and bake for 25 minutes. Uncover and bake until bubbling, 5 to 10 minutes more.

••• Tip

Frozen spinach contains a lot of water, which, if not removed, can ruin a recipe. To extract the excess moisture, place the thawed block of spinach in a colander to drain, then press down on it or squeeze it with your hands.

shortcut meals

SESAME CHICKEN SALAD

hands-on time: 15 minutes | total time: 15 minutes | makes 4 servings

2 carrots

2 5-ounce bags baby spinach

1 small red onion, thinly sliced

3 tablespoons sesame seeds, toasted

1 store-bought rotisserie chicken, meat shredded

1 1-inch piece fresh ginger, grated

2 tablespoons low-sodium soy sauce

2 tablespoons rice vinegar

1/4 cup sesame oil

Using a vegetable peeler, shave the carrots into long, thin ribbons. In a large bowl, combine the carrots, spinach, onion, sesame seeds, and chicken. In a separate bowl, whisk together the ginger, soy sauce, and vinegar. Whisking constantly, slowly add the oil in a steady stream. Pour the vinaigrette over the salad and toss to coat. Divide among individual plates and serve.

and the next time, try...
Assembling this salad with shredded lettuce in place of the baby spinach for a crunchier texture—and a more kid-friendly taste.

···Tip
Toasting brings out the nutty flavor of sesame seeds. Heat them in a dry skillet over medium heat, stirring the seeds or shaking the pan frequently, for 1 to 2 minutes. Watch the seeds carefully; they can go from lightly toasted to scorched in seconds.

SHRIMP WITH ARUGULA AND COUSCOUS

hands-on time: 15 minutes | total time: 15 minutes | makes 4 servings

1 cup instant couscous
3/4 teaspoon kosher salt
1/8 teaspoon black pepper
3 tablespoons olive oil
1 clove garlic, thinly sliced
1 5-ounce bag arugula
1 1-pound bag frozen uncooked shrimp, thawed
1 lemon, cut into wedges

Prepare the couscous according to the package directions. After cooking, season it with 1/4 teaspoon of the salt and a pinch of the pepper. Meanwhile, heat 2 tablespoons of the oil in a large skillet over medium heat. Add the garlic and cook for 1 minute. Add the arugula and cook just until wilted, about 1 minute. Transfer to a plate. Rinse the shrimp and pat them dry with paper towels. Heat the remaining oil in the skillet over medium-high heat. Add the shrimp, lemon wedges, and the remaining salt and pepper. Cook, turning once, until the shrimp are pink and cooked through, about 4 minutes total. Return the garlic and arugula to the skillet and toss. Serve over the couscous.

•••• Tip

Arugula has a peppery flavor and a fairly hearty texture that stand up well to a brief stint in the skillet. If you prefer something a little milder in flavor, try spinach.

shortcut meals

FRENCH FRY PIE

hands-on time: 15 minutes | total time: 40 minutes | makes 4 servings

1 28-ounce package frozen
shoestring French fries
1 1/2 pounds ground beef
1 14- to 16-ounce jar pasta sauce
1/2 teaspoon kosher salt

Heat oven to 425° F. Spread the fries on a baking sheet. Bake until golden, about 25 minutes. Meanwhile, cook the beef in a medium saucepan over medium heat, crumbling it with a spoon, until no trace of pink remains, about 7 minutes. Spoon off and discard any excess fat. Stir in the pasta sauce and cook until warmed through, about 5 minutes. Transfer to an 8-inch-square baking dish or a 9-inch deep-dish pie plate. Top with the fries and return to oven for 5 to 10 minutes. Season with the salt. Spoon into individual bowls.

•••Tip
Is dinner ready before your family is? Like most casseroles, the French Fry Pie can remain in the oven for at least 15 additional minutes while everyone meanders to the table.

MEDITERRANEAN CHICKEN

hands-on time: 20 minutes | total time: 30 minutes | makes 4 servings

$1/2$ cup (2 ounces) crumbled Feta

4 tablespoons black-olive tapenade or paste

4 boneless, skinless chicken breast halves

$1/2$ teaspoon black pepper

3 tablespoons olive oil

$1/2$ cup store-bought salsa (preferably fresh), drained

1 5-ounce bag baby spinach

4 tablespoons capers (optional)

1 lemon, cut into wedges

Heat oven to 375° F. Combine the Feta and tapenade in a small bowl. Rinse the chicken and pat it dry with paper towels. With a sharp knife, make a 2-inch slit in the thickest part of each chicken breast half to form a pocket. Using a spoon, stuff some of the Feta mixture into each pocket. Season the chicken with the pepper. Heat 2 tablespoons of the oil in a nonstick skillet over medium heat. Add the chicken and cook until browned, about 2 minutes per side. Transfer to a baking dish and bake until cooked through, about 15 minutes. Meanwhile, heat the remaining oil and the salsa in the skillet over medium heat until warmed through, about 5 minutes. Add the spinach and cook, tossing frequently, until barely wilted, about 1 minute. Place the spinach and salsa on individual plates, top with the chicken, and sprinkle with the capers, if desired. Serve the lemon wedges on the side.

•••Tip

If you don't have enough chicken on hand to serve everyone an individual piece, cut the chicken crosswise into slices and fan them out on the plates. No one will know the difference.

shortcut meals

HAM-AND-CHEESE WAFFLE SANDWICHES

hands-on time: 10 minutes | total time: 20 minutes | makes 4 servings

8 frozen plain or whole-grain
  toaster waffles, unthawed
1 tablespoon Dijon mustard
  (optional)
1/2 pound sliced deli ham
1/4 pound Cheddar, thinly sliced
4 tablespoons unsalted butter

Place 4 of the waffles on a work surface. Spread with the mustard (if using). Top with the ham, Cheddar, and the remaining waffles. Spread the top of each sandwich with 1/2 tablespoon of the butter. Melt the remaining butter in a large non-stick skillet over medium heat. Place the sandwiches in the skillet, buttered-side up. Cook, pressing with the back of a spatula and turning occasionally, until the Cheddar melts and the waffles are golden, 3 to 4 minutes per side.

and the next time, try...
Switching up the fillings with other pantry and refrigerator staples:
• Turkey, mozzarella, and honey mustard
• Peanut butter and jelly
• Scrambled eggs and Swiss cheese

••• Tip
Looking to get some mileage out of your neglected waffle iron? Use it to put a new face— a dimpled one at that— on sandwiches made with plain sliced bread.

SPICY CHICKEN AND TORTILLA SOUP

hands-on time: 20 minutes | total time: 40 minutes | makes 4 servings

1 store-bought rotisserie chicken
2 32-ounce containers low-sodium chicken broth
1 small red onion, finely chopped
2 jalapeños, seeded and thinly sliced
2 large tomatoes, seeded and diced
1 cup corn kernels, thawed if frozen, or fresh (from 2 ears)
A couple of handfuls of tortilla chips ½ cup fresh cilantro leaves
1 ripe avocado, roughly chopped
1 cup (4 ounces) crumbled Feta
1 lime, cut into wedges

Remove and discard the skin from the chicken. Place the entire chicken and the broth in a large pot over medium heat. Simmer for 20 minutes. Transfer the chicken to a plate to cool. Strain the broth into another saucepan. Shred the chicken meat and add it to the broth, along with the onion, jalapeños, and tomatoes and their juices. Place over medium heat and cook for 5 minutes. Add the corn and heat until warmed through, about 3 minutes. Place some of the tortilla chips in each bowl. Ladle in the soup and top with the cilantro, avocado, Feta, and the remaining chips. Serve the lime wedges on the side.

••• Tip

Among hot peppers, jalapeños fall in the medium-spicy range. If you prefer something certifiably hot, substitute serrano or Thai red chili peppers.

recipe index

a

antipasto plate 134–135
artichokes, linguine with leeks and 54–55
arugula
  in grilled tuna with tomato salsa 58–59
  in pork chops with lemony
    bread crumbs 62–63
  shrimp with arugula
    and couscous 142–143
asparagus, in steamed halibut in
parchment 28–29

b

barley, in mushroom barley soup . . . 116–117
beans
  baked 20–21
  chickpea salad with spiced
    lamb chops 78–79
  and pasta 120–121
  tuna and white bean salad 36–37
beef
  and beer stew 10–11
  classic beef stew 124–125
  in French fry pie 144–145
  in lasagna-style baked ziti 118–119
  in not-so-sloppy joes 70–71
  in pasta with Bolognese sauce 106–107
  soy-marinated London broil 68–69
  steak with root vegetables 52–53
beets, in steak with root vegetables 52–53
blue cheese, in chicken salad with
  peaches and 86–87
bread, in panzanella 98–99
bresaola, in antipasto plate 134–135
broccoli, in vegetable soup 14–15
broccoli rabe, in pasta with broccoli
  rabe and sausage 76–77
butternut squash soup 108–109

c

cabbage
  green, in grilled shrimp tacos 56–57
  Napa, in inside-out spring rolls 136–137
cantaloupe soup 84–85
carrots
  in chicken potpie 130–131
  in classic beef stew 124–125
  in inside-out spring rolls 136–137
  in lamb tagine with olives
    and lemon 18–19
  in mushroom barley soup 116–117
  in roast chicken and vegetables 8–9
  in sesame chicken salad 140–141
  in smoky split-pea soup 112–113
  in steak with root vegetables 52–53
  in turkey noodle soup 126–127
Cheddar cheese
  French toast with sizzled tomatoes . . 42–43
  ham-and-cheese waffle
    sandwiches 148–149
  macaroni and cheese 110–111
chicken
  cacciatore 24–25
  curry 114–115
  cutlets with herb sauce 60–61
  Mediterranean chicken 146–147
  Parmesan-crusted chicken cutlets . . . 38–39
  potpie 130–131
  roast chicken with olives
    and thyme 30–31
  roast chicken and vegetables 8–9
  salad with peaches
    and blue cheese 86–87
  sesame chicken salad 140–141
  souvlaki 64–65
  spicy chicken and tortilla soup 150–151
chickpeas, in spiced lamb chops with
  chickpea salad 78–79

cod, in roast cod with crisp potatoes . . . 16–17
corn
  fluffy corn and goat
    cheese omelets 34–35
  scallop and corn chowder 12–13
couscous
  lamb tagine with couscous 18–19
  shrimp with arugula
    and couscous 142–143
cucumber, in smoked salmon with
  cucumber and watercress 88–89
curry, in chicken curry 114–115

e

eggplant, in cheesy vegetable
pasta 122–123
eggs
  fluffy corn and goat
    cheese omelets 34–35
  saucy eggs 46–47

f

fennel
  in gazpacho 100–101
  roast salmon, fennel,
    and red onion 22–23
Feta cheese
  in cheesy vegetable pasta 122–123
  in chicken souvlaki 64–65
  in Greek salad 94–95
  in Mediterranean chicken 146–147
fish (See also *seafood*)
  grilled tuna with tomato salsa 58–59
  pan bagnat 96–97
  poached halibut with green beans
    and red potatoes 74–75
  roast cod with crisp potatoes 16–17

recipe index

tip index

credits

MEALS MADE EASY

Food Stylist Stephana Bottom
Prop Stylist Philippa Brathwaite

REAL SIMPLE

Managing Editor Kristin van Ogtrop
Creative Director Vanessa Holden
Special Projects Editor Sarah Humphreys
Design Director, Special Projects Eva Spring
Copy Editor Myles McDonnell
Research Editor Westry Green
Food Director Frances Boswell
Food Editor Renee Schettler
Photo Editor Naomi Nista
Senior Designer Carolyn Veith Krienke
Editorial Assistant Amanda Armstrong
Recipe Tester Simon Andrews

Publisher Steven Sachs
Associate Publisher, Advertising Kevin White
General Manager Karen Saltser Cohen
Consumer Marketing Director Kristiana Helmick
Vice President, PR and Communications
Kristen Jones Connell

President, Corporate Media and Marketing
Robin Domeniconi

TIME INC. HOME ENTERTAINMENT

Publisher Richard Fraiman
Executive Director, Marketing Services Carol Pittard
Director, Retail & Special Sales Tom Mifsud
Marketing Director, Branded Businesses Swati Rao
Director, New Product Development Peter Harper
Financial Director Steven Sandonato
Assistant General Counsel Dasha Smith Dwin
Prepress Manager Emily Rabin
Book Production Manager Suzanne Janso
Product Manager Victoria Alfonso
Associate Prepress Manager
Anne-Michelle Gallero

SPECIAL THANKS

Bozena Bannett, Vanessa Boer, John Boswell, Ryan Bourquin, Glenn Buonocore, Kay Chun, Alick Crossley, Diane Fields, Jean Galton, Alex Grant, Pamela Grossman, Aundrea King, Jane Kirby, Emma Knowles, Noirin Lucas, Robert Marasco, Cyd Raftus McDowell, Brooke McGuire, Frank Mentesana, Kate Merker, Jacklyn Monk, Nancy Negovetich, Cynthia Nicholson, Barbara Noris, Peter Occolowitz, Leslie Pendleton, Jonathan Polsky, Alex Press, Sara Quessenberry, Chavaughn Raines, Ilene Schreider, Nina Simonds, Katy Sparks, Kelly Staikopoulos, Susie Theodorou, Adriana Tierno, Suzy Verrier, Dierdre Ward, Britney Williams.

SPECIAL THANKS TO THE FOLLOWING STORES
Aero, Armani Casa, Calvin Klein Home, Takashimaya.

First printing April 2006

Printed in China

We welcome your comments and suggestions about *Real Simple* Books. Please e-mail us at books@realsimple.com, or write to us at:
REAL SIMPLE BOOKS
1271 AVENUE OF THE AMERICAS
ROOM 4139
NEW YORK, NY 10020

If you would like to order any of our hardcover-edition books, please call us at 800-327-6388 (Monday through Friday, 7:00 A.M. to 8:00 P.M. Central Time; or Saturday, 7:00 A.M. to 6:00 P.M. Central Time).